# *Love* and
# Illusion

*Are you married or dating a sociopath?*

*A chilling fact:*

*1 in 25 adults now carry sociopathic traits*

*How would you know?*

By

## Sheila Z. Stirling, Ph.D.

*My Dear Friend Elta shinning star I love & honor you*

# *Testimonials*

This is a 'must read' for every woman who is dating or has ever been betrayed in a relationship. This eye opening book is unique also in that it is a healing journey, regaining the ability to trust yourself and your judgment. A powerful message in a few words.

**–Elissa MacLachlan, PhD, MhD, Transpersonal Psychologist**

"A powerful account of toxic relationships with real psychopaths, (sociopaths) including the illusions they create and how to dispel them."

**— Patricia Evans, Author, "Controlling People"**

This book can save you the heartbreak, Chilling and disturbing as it is. Every woman must read " Love and Illusion" **–Beth**

" If I had read this book at age 23 I would have had a very different life. This hit home for me as I now know I was married to a "Social Sociopath" it lasted 5 years and my life was in shambles especially my self esteem and feeling like I was "the crazy one". My life is changed for the better after reading your book. Thank you for bringing the hidden darkness into the light. Thank you for helping me to know I can put my life back together. Thank you" **– Leslie**

Love and Illusion was a perfect read for me. An emotional ride that speaks to both the left and right brain.
I just loved the balance of science and true life stories. I sat down and read this in one take.. I was impressed that you laid out a clear path to re empowering anyone who has been through a "relation" with one of these "social sociopaths." Brilliant Sheila Just Brilliant, **– Elta**

Published by Wisdom Press Publishing

4132 S. Rainbow Blvd. #465, Las Vegas NV, 89103 USA
ISBN13: 978-0-9778891-7-4
ISBN 10: 0-9778891-7-3
June 2010

Library of Congress Cataloging – in – publication Data
Stirling Sheila Z
Web site: www.wisdompresspublishing.com

Cover Art by D'ziner Graphics, dziner@comcast.net
Co-Edited by Dianne Leonetti, dziner@comcast.net

Note from the author and publisher:
This publication is designed to provide accurate information with regard to the subject matter. The information in this book is not meant in any way to diagnose or replace medical advice or treatment.

This book is available at quantity discounts for bulk purchase.

For information call: 1-866-612-7051

**Visit us at www.WisdomPressPublishing.com**

Printed in the United States of America

# Table of Contents

# Foreword

---

Love, all you need is love, love makes the world go round, love can change the world, love can make a poor man rich and turn sorrow to joy. All well-known words and ones we have said and sung for years. All our life we have been shown, told, and taught "To love is to know the truth of your soul."

Love permeates every cell, every thought, every intent, and every action. Love is gentle, love is kind, and love is patient and understanding. Love cares and hearts swoon, our eyes twinkle, how wonderful and sincere each and every love is. The feeling when you are in love cannot be matched by any other feeling on this beautiful planet.

I believe in every word above, but now I must ask the question:
### *Is it Love or Illusion?*

Recently many have seen the chilling story of what I refer to as the "purest Sociopath," such as the story of Joran Van Der Sloot. The young Dutch playboy who allegedly murdered a young woman because she looked him up on the Internet. It is now looking like there may be more than one beautiful young woman murdered. First a confession and then a denial.

***Have you ever thought:*** Oh! That would never happen to me? Let me ask you: Could you have avoided this person? Could you have spotted the underlying rage? Could you have seen through the easygoing smile, and charming armor that is so eloquently staged knowingly or unknowingly by Joran Der Sloot?

From my experience, if you are thinking, "Yes! I could have seen through all the smoke and mirrors, through all the mask's and that could never happen to me," you are in good company and yes, that is an illusion.

This book is full of references, facts and research. But, what makes this writing unique is that a survivor wrote it. All the stories included herein are written by survivors in their own words.

I admit that I became so intrigued and entangled by the "unbelievable behavior and disregard" of my partner that the last year of this crazy "relationship" was for research, and yes, desperately backing my way out, while forcing myself to look at the reality of the situation. It is rare indeed that someone can have a conversation with a Sociopath about Sociopathic behavior. To remain genuinely cool and calm is unusual. To show no emotion and discuss lies, deceit, infidelity, and betrayal of all sorts. That is what had to be done in order to have some truth shared. I had to make myself seem like an extension of his game, like what he was doing was fascinating to me and by that time it was true. The relationship had somehow turned into a research project and I was twisted up inside it. It's a world I hope you never have to step into. But, if you are reading this, you probably have experienced someone on some level who carries these traits.

Yes, my personal experience is woven into this writing, and this book speaks to all and hopefully will help the reader that may be involved with, or near to someone carrying the traits of a "social sociopath." The flags and signs are not what one would expect and, are so very important to know. If some of what you read rings a bell, sounds off an alarm, reminds you of someone you may be dating, engaged to or married to, this is your cue to wake up! Know this relationship will end badly for you because an addict only loves his addiction and the sociopath is addicted to his or her own ability to win the game. They want to control, to fulfill their self-serving agenda and this has nothing to do with you or how wonderful you are. Take heed that you are just a pawn in their game, and if you have a heart it will certainly be broken.

As you explore the stories in this writing, search your own situation and look into your own life to see if you are experiencing some similar circumstances or perhaps have a friend, family member or someone at the office that can make good use of this information. This writing will explore different stories that illustrate the differences between Love and Illusion. The case studies written in Love and Illusion are true; every word is true. For the purpose of protecting families and members of families who are involved; the names of all individuals have been changed.

# Acknowledgements

---

One must write about what one knows. What one has experienced and felt. Not only from the viewpoint of a therapist, patient, or from a perspective of a viewer, but as someone who has gone through it and experienced every aspect of the subject, lived it, really been in it and lived through it and is well qualified to write the story down and to be of service to others. I would like to say a heartfelt thank you to my support team. You know who you are. I called and cried on your shoulder, day and night needing to talk about it as I worked it out in my own being. I know you got so tired of hearing about it and I thank you for your love, your kindness and patience with me. I am so grateful for your caring and support. You are my heroes and I salute you. I would like to acknowledge the brave women who came forward with their stories to share their own experiences of this dismantling behavior.

As much as it pains me to say it, I must acknowledge the Social Sociopath whom I knew for almost five years, fell in love with and lived with for more than two and a half years. He was a catalyst for change and the inspiration for this book.

I also would like to acknowledge the countless unsung heroes who have survived through a "sociopathic relationship." You know who you are; you have been lied to, cheated on, manipulated, emotionally, verbally and sometimes even physically abused, you have thought you were the crazy one, it was your fault and somehow you were left in a mess, with shattered dreams, shattered lives and bewildered beyond belief. You need to know that you are not the crazy one. This disaster was not about you and you need not take responsibility for it. In this writing we will unravel the mystery behind the behavior. Yes, these social predators are out there, beautiful and charming. To know them is fun and alluring, to love them and allow them to love you is disaster.

# Author's notes

This is the time of a great evolution. Our world is changing every moment. Is this not our time to shine? To seek the truth in all we do and all we are? Are we not ushering in the new age of understanding and is this not the time we must all take responsibility for the human form we are in? Pardon me, but I have it on very good authority that this is the time of the great shift! The time we can all feel peace within and love throughout the galaxy. The hundredth monkey is almost getting it and we are so close to a wondrous tomorrow we can see it and feel it and sense it.

So, what is going on with this up cropping of beings who live only for themselves and seek and destroy all we know to hold dear? Such as our inter-personal relationships with each other, our sincere caring and sharing. I believe everything is for a reason and there are no coincidences. So, if everything is in divine timing, then my collision with one of these creatures was no accident. I am grateful for the eye-opening experience. I am grateful for falling in love. I am still recovering from the vast emotional upheaval and sadness of the disappointment, but I will be fine. Just give me some time. I have broken free from the illusion and so I write the truth for the benefit of all. If we are to open our hearts to the evolution of our species it may be very important to know some of the hidden places and the secrets of those who would hunt for the game and live for the kill and then move on to the next.

# Introduction

This book is for everyone as it will define, describe, and explain sociopathic behavior in adults. It is not as rare as we would hope it would be. Today, one in every 25 adults are sailing through life with this behavior, reeking havoc and breaking hearts and spirits for all who cross their path. If you become too close and even worse, fall in love with one of these beautiful and dangerous creatures and believe what they think and say is real (when in fact it is an illusion), your world will be tumbling down. For it is a well thought out game for the enjoyment of the wearer of these abusive traits. Some say these are just selfish people, players or playboys looking to use others for their own personal gain, for money, status, and sexual pleasures or just to see if they can once again "win the game." In some cases this may be true, a careful evaluation of the 20 traits will separate the spoiled child from the cunning social predator. There is a vast difference; history and pattern do come into consideration when evaluating your specific situation.

The stories and examples are all written by women. We all know that gender is only one factor in this stunning unveiling of this brutal behavior. It is mostly men who carry these traits but there are a much smaller number of women who knowingly or unknowingly are acting out the social sociopathic life as well.

This is a particularly dismantling and subtle type of abuse. It may take some time to even realize you are in the "victim" arena, as many of us absolutely do not view ourselves as victims at all. It happens slowly sometimes, a harsh look or word in the beginning, a discounting of what you do or who you are. A lack of empathy or kindness on their part, and yet you sometimes do not even see this behavior as abuse. It is confusing and you do not sense right away that you are being manipulated, played out like a game. The abuser, the one carrying these traits, is often seen as the most charismatic and charming person. Your friends and family may think he is wonderful and look at you as if you were somehow causing the "upset" in your relationship. They have no idea what goes on behind the magic curtain.

Love and Illusion will give you a heads up of Red Flags and sincere words of wisdom you can use and pass on. A roadway back to yourself, to reclaiming your power and your joyous life once again. It is impossible to imagine the devastation these social predators can leave in their wake.

*"Three things cannot be long hidden: the sun, the moon, and the truth"*

**Hindu Prince Siddhartha,**
**the founder of Buddhism 563 – 483 B.C.**

# CHAPTER 1

## Sociopaths Among Us

When you hear the word "Sociopath" what comes to mind? A movie you once saw where the villain was pure evil, had no conscience and ran around sawing people in two or became a crazed murderer? If you think this is not real just take a look at recent ABC news. It reads: "Peruvian authorities are pressuring Joran Van Der Sloot to give them information about the disappearance of Natalie Holloway in the wake of the Dutch playboy's reported confession that he murdered a 21-year-old Peruvian woman, Stephanie Flores Ramirez. After five days of denying his involvement in any way the 22-year-old, Joran admitted to the authorities that he grabbed her by the neck and hit her."

Joran was said to be tearful as he told police, "I had to do it because she was intruding in my private life." Apparently, Ms. Ramirez had read some information about Joran on the Internet and that was enough of a trigger to justify him taking her life. You can read more about this chilling story by Googling Joran Van Der Sloot. This is the typical Sociopath, cleverly disguised as a young playboy, out in society and living among us. For those of us who have been around a while, we can also remember Ted Bundy, charming mass murderer, and Hannibal Lecter, the chilling account of this man was made into a horrifying movie: "Silence of the Lambs." This is how most of us think or believe all sociopaths are. For some, this would be true but, what of the majority of these people who secretly live their life among us, as a social predator? Society has led us to believe that this is a "rare" disorder and is easy to spot. After all, these are people who have no conscience, no moral boundaries and no remorse. They make their own rules, and do not live in society. Right? Wrong!

If you Google "sociopath" there is only one definition with approximately 20 characteristics. I believe there are multiple <u>levels</u> of sociopathic behavior. It is through my own research and observation that the term "Social Sociopath" was born. There is a distinct difference in the two behaviors.

The underlying causes are similar, but how the syndrome motivates and plays out is basically one of two ways:
> 1. The Purest Sociopath
> 2. The Social Sociopath

**Let's explore the similarities as well as the differences.**
Perhaps in the future we will further define more categories of the sociopathic behavior but for now we will explore the two mentioned above. I define one as he "Purest Sociopath" and the other as the "Social Sociopath." It is the Social Sociopath we will be talking about in this writing.

**Let's distinguish the Purest from the Social Sociopath:**
The Purest Sociopath has not learned to control their rage and total lack of feeling for life itself. He or she acts out without the slightest remorse; they can stab you in the heart while looking in your eyes just to see the expression

you have in your last breath. They feel totally superior to "humans" and so have little regard for life, liberty and the pursuit of happiness, of course, unless it is their own. We have been led to believe all sociopaths are like this; they stick out like a sore thumb and we all know to stay away. If you feel safe in your world and believe these creatures are so easy to spot and of course they would never be someone in your circle, then you have bought into the illusion and that is a dangerous place to be. Due to the sometimes radical behavior of the Purest Sociopath, most are destined to a life of violence and probable constant run-ins with the law. We feel safer at night knowing these emotionless creatures are put away, keeping the rest of us from harms way.

The key component to the difference between the "purest" and the "social" sociopath is in the method of acting out. The purest sociopath erases or has no boundary that keeps him from physically and brutally acting out on others. The "social sociopath" has a boundary that keeps him from being physically abusive to others. When that line is crossed or the boundary is blurred, you may have a full-blown Sociopath on your hands. This would be the time to use the nearest exit.

What I call the "Social Sociopath" is another story altogether. A not-so-new kid on the block; they are someone whom, over the years has become a master of the "Game." They live, eat, breathe, work, play, and conduct their lives among us, blending in for the most part. Except for the fact that they usually leave a messy and devastating trail behind them. It does not seem fair that the nicest, friendliest person at the local pub could be one of these "conscienceless" creatures.

They have pushed the anger and rage way down so that most people only see the sweetest smile, the nicest guy. They are helpful, fun and generous, and so charming that everyone wants to know them. This social predator is the most dangerous of all because he fits right in, often as the life of the party, the one who opens the door for you or offers to carry your groceries in for you. Most of us in society will come in contact with this kind of Sociopath at some point. It truly does not make him or her less dangerous, it just appears that way to all of us. Lack of remorse and feelings of superiority make all people who carry sociopathic behavior potentially volatile and dangerous.

The common thread of both types of sociopath is the unresolved and underlying rage they carry. An unrealized part of themselves, usually from an overbearing or controlling father figure or a mother that just did not have time to bond, will cause this emotional detachment. Yes, even before they can walk or talk, this behavior starts as a coping mechanism for the infant, a built-in self-preservation chip is activated and so it begins.

The Social Sociopath appears to fit into society; some become leaders, and head up thriving companies. But, usually lose that which they thought they wanted, or had, due to this is part of the pattern, once they feel they have "conquered" the situation, they are compelled to move on unconsciously (or consciously) destroying what they have built, whether it pertains to friends, family or even business. Their nomadic drive is strong and they live only for their own purpose and gratification, desperately trying to fill the hollowness inside where most of us feel caring and deeper emotions. Their life is one deception after another, all of life is a game, all people are pawns in their game and the only true feeling is reserved for themselves. Yes, they are in your circles, perhaps in your home, or in your work place. One in every 25 adults in this country carries some of these traits, and it is males – three-to-one, who dominate this subcategory of the human species.

# Description of a Social Sociopath

This is a person that looks like you or me. Usually they are appealing to the eye, and it is impossible to see these traits on the outside without knowing exactly what you are looking for. Not every charming person is a sociopath, not every love is a game, but it is important that we do pay attention or we will pay the price.

Because Social Sociopaths live among us, they blend in; they may be successful, classy, and charismatic and oh, so charming, intelligent, and manipulative. They have a high need for stimulation and are masters of seduction. Somehow, they seem so exciting and intense in all they do. They are missing a conscience, have no guilt or remorse. They capture hearts and souls, they hunt and when they have conquered their prey, they laugh, wipe the drool from their mouth and move on, leaving all kinds of devastation in their wake. This pattern used to be called "Moral Insanity." I think that is a close description.

A sociopath does not have the ability to love anyone and usually that includes him or herself. They have learned the motions of love and it feels very real.

It is hard for us to imagine that there are people whom carry this trait of having no guilt or conscious, no real empathy for another. Conscience and boundaries make up a good portion of our lives, and that mechanism is what makes us human. Conscience is tied directly to our emotional ties with others. Putting another's need or wants before our own, or taking the feeling of another into the very fabric of our choice making is what love and friendship is all about.

The sociopath may throw himself into work having a deep commitment to his chosen industry because it requires no personal attachment and this may be an area where he is most comfortable as long as he is in a position of control, all things will sail smoothly, seemingly tireless and driven in both work and social environments. It is an illusion yet, can be a motivation for someone carrying sociopathic traits that "to dominate is a worthwhile goal" and to have "moral exclusion" viewing all others as merely human while seeing themselves as super human.

The social sociopath male does best to stay single. The problem is, he is addicted to the euphoria of "new love" and to the hunt. He may have six, eight, or even more women at any given time. But, there will always be the favorite one or two "loves" and then he may find someone really intriguing. He feels like he is falling in love, and for the moment the hollow place fills full and he will marry or move in with his special one knowing that he will continue to hunt. Living a secret life is one of the key components for this social predator to stay put for the time being, for he is being re-quickened, and to us it looks and feels like real love.

***An example:*** In the upcoming case study it states "even on a first date our charismatic predator knew this woman fit his criteria for the re-quickening; well-dressed and well-educated, owned a home and was well respected in the community. Successful and well liked, he was compelled to pursue her because she looked like a prize to him. A worthy opponent, a good challenge.

## *This example is from my own personal story:*

"We were out to dinner on our very first date and he just stared at me with pure love in his eyes and said "Oh, I am so smitten." (This meant he really liked me and now had to make the choice to continue courting and hunting me or let me go. The actual words were very different and changed for the book as to not offend the readers. If you would like to know the real words just email me and I will be happy to share.) His choice was to continue courting me, I was oh so willing for at this point he seemed to be a wonderful companion and it felt like there was real potential for "love."

And then one day, weeks or months later when he saw the look of love in my eyes back to him, he said to me: "Oh, you are so in trouble." It was probably six or seven months before I said, "I love you." His reply was, "You are so in trouble!" (It sounded like a playful moment and that is how it was said but perhaps it was an unconscious warning.

We would both laugh but it was no laughing matter and certainly the truth. The Social Sociopath appears so cute, always laughing and smiling: cute like a baby rattlesnake 10 times more poisonous than their parents.

In *"The Sociopath Next Door"* by Martha Stout, PhD, the author described it like this:

"Sociopaths are noted especially for their shallowness of emotion, the hollow and transient nature of any affectionate feeling they may claim to have, a certain breathtaking callousness. They have no trace of empathy and no genuine interest in bonding emotionally with a mate. Once the surface charm is scraped off, their marriages are loveless, one sided, and almost always short term. A mate may have value as a possession but he is never sad or accountable."

This statement is true. Devastatingly true.

A sociopath is usually narcissistic, sex addicted, alcohol addicted, emotionally abusive, verbally abusive and just out to have fun, fun, fun! That is for him or her, of course. If you can add to the fun you are the greatest while the fun lasts.

A note about the female social sociopath: Using her false mask, this charming "Southern Belle" schemer appears helpless or needy, pitiful, inept, or emotionally unable to cope. Even total strangers give her things and she gratefully accepts. Falsely claiming to be the victim, this passive parasite lures and abuses the normal protector/ provider instincts in her male target. When her mask comes off she is cunning, ruthless, predatory, and loveless. This is stated by Lisa Scott (info in index).

Please let it be noted that not all Social Sociopaths indulge in alcohol, and some may not carry all the 20 traits that are in the Hare check list coming up after our first case study. Many of the behaviors listed below will not even show until one gets "close." To the outside world these charmers seem to be the most charismatic people around, knowledgeable and kind.

*"It's a man's actions that define him"*

**Professor Doubletree - Harry Potter**

# CHAPTER 2

---

## Our first case study:
## "Back Away from My Heart"

As the author of this book using the name "Sheri" allows me to present a clearer view of my story. It also feels good to be a bit removed from it.

I wanted this story to be the last story but the editor insisted that this was one of the milder stories and needed to be first so, here it is.

(This is the true story of falling in love with a Social Sociopath. For me "Sheri" it was the dream, the dream come true, the illusion, the nightmare, the awakening, and recovery. For Steven it was the search, the hunt, the quickening, the pattern, the switch, and the blizzard.)

Before you begin reading this story it is important to understand the dynamic of this relationship. When Steven and I entered into a relationship we actually sat down and discussed how we wanted it to be. Steven said he wanted a monogamous, committed relationship with me, I was not so sure about that. I said to him "are you sure this is what you want?" I knew he had a reputation for being a flirt and this was not a threat for me and I was okay if we both had friends of the opposite sex. Steven was very sure he wanted total exclusivity with me. So we agreed. I did not twist his arm to make this agreement. In fact, it was he who had to convince me it was time to be a couple. I was very clear and let him know that the one thing I must have in order to be in a relationship with him was "Rigorous Honesty." I said, "You can say anything to me as long as it is the truth."

For me, I would be honest and monogamous, because integrity, sacred trust, and honesty are choices. Steven knew he could be honest with me without the thought of repercussions. I made it very clear, that in our life together, I had to be the one he made his alliance with; the one he talked to and shared his life and his truth with. He had the perfect place to experience life the way he chose to but he chose to lie and cheat on a daily basis. For an example, he would call and say he was somewhere when he was really somewhere else! He told me he could not get reception at his jobsite but the phone bill showed he called many other women all day long, day after day, and then he would come home and say how hard it was to not be able to talk to anyone all day. When given the choice to be honorable he chose always to disregard his own words and agreements, and chose to lie, cheat, manipulate, and deceive. I was very naive then to what I know now.

Social Sociopaths have their own rules and although, when you are the focus of their affection there is nothing like it. They wine and dine you, take you shopping and buy you wonderful gifts. Hold onto you like you are breath itself, build you up and seem to genuinely be interested in all you do and all you feel and who you are. They feel like the "perfect mate"… in the beginning.

It was late 2005 and a friend of a friend was having a party. It was one of those special parties where you had to be shuttled from a meeting place up to the home. The party was lavish with exotic foods and showgirls from the Las Vegas Strip, as well as some well-known entertainers and locals. Still, after an hour or so I felt a bit bored so, I said good night to the few people I knew and headed for the door. As I was walking out a gentleman, fairly good looking, was also walking out. He was heading to his car, which was parked right in front of the house! "Wow," he must be special because he is the only one parked in front of the house. He offered me a ride to my car and I said "Oh, yes, thank you!" He opened the passenger side door of his silver Mercedes, I said thank you and got in the car, made myself comfortable as he shut the door and walked around to the driver's side. He got in, shut the door and then he stopped, turned and looked at me very seriously and said, "I cannot believe you just got into a car with a total stranger!"

Without missing a beat and with a very serious look on my face I said, "Are you a murderer?" He laughed and said NO! So, I said, "Then take me to my car, please," which he did and we had a witty conversation on the way. He told me he was divorced and that it was very complicated. I listened and as I was getting out of his car he gave me his number but I never did call him. (By the way, years later he confessed to me that his leaving the party at the same time as I was no accident. He was watching me and decided to check me out.)

About a year later we saw each other at another party and we seemed to be drawn to each other. He came right over and we started a great conversation. We talked and laughed and he walked me to my car and opened the door. The perfect gentleman. He called me a few times and we had long and great conversations. It was months later when a friend called. I believe it was a Tuesday. Steven was over at her house fixing her closet. (He is always so helpful to casual "friends.") She put him on the phone and we had an uplifting conversation. He said, "I hear you do not want a relationship!" I said, "That is correct. I am very busy, very happy and have a full life!" His reply was, "Great! Will you have dinner with me this Friday eve?" My answer was yes and so it began!

We seemed to just get along in everything we did. On our very first date he kept looking at me and saying, "I am so smitten with you." We began spending more time together and it was incredible. We fit like a glove. Each week we seemed to want to be together more and more. We had a blast, dining and dancing, walking, kissing, hugging, hours of wonderful conversations, you name it – we did it. We traveled well together and took many short vacations together. We got along like we were meant for each other, a perfect fit. (That was my illusion.) I had known him over two years and wouldn't you think that a man who was married for 14 years is OKAY???? Well, there is also the fact he had been married six times so that in retrospect needed to be a "Flag" and I just ignored it. I thought he must have grown up some, as he shared with me how he was so devastated when the woman he left his 14-year marriage for... dumped him. (Little did I know at that time all these women *or most of them,* were still very much in his life, his secret life). We had a wonderful carefree seven months of dating and spending almost every moment together. He used to say, "I don't like myself, and I'm messed up." But, I had no idea how messed up he was, since I had not encountered a full-blown Social Sociopath before – at least not one that was in my personal world. That was another warning I did not heed. The feeling of belonging and being in love was so overwhelming for me. I had my eyes wide shut! A poster child for "love is blind."

One of our short trips was to visit my family in California. They just loved Steven, everybody got along so well, and it felt like they accepted Steven far more than they accepted me. I was thrilled and thought, "Oh, my family loves him too. He must be the perfect mate for me!"

I was married once, many years ago and, yes, my ex-husband had affairs and lied but I believe he had a conscience, he had remorse, and I want to believe he felt guilt. However, it gets you thinking… "My God, are they all like this?" The answer is, no, they are not all like this.

Steven courted me for over a year and we became great friends (or so I thought). The time came and he was looking for a place to move into. He said he had been renting a room in someone's home and needed to now find his own place. I had never been invited there and had no idea where it was and, looking back, that was a red flag.

He said, "I love you and we get along so well." We sat down like two adults and made a detailed plan. Steven wanted to move in with me and help financially, so we went over the bills just like real people might do in a long-term relationship.

I had been single for many years so, I really put some thought into what was happening. This was not something I would just jump into. We talked about it for weeks and we had been dating and seeing each other every day for almost a year. I thought "he is so special," he is gentle and kind, loves to have fun, and seems to accept me for who I am. He was wonderful and supportive, and I was falling in love with him. Romantically, or should I say sexually, he was intense and liked it rough in the bedroom sometimes, but it still seemed normal, if there is such a thing as "normal." Steven loved to take me shopping and actually would sit for hours and watch while I got my hair done, he was just happy to be near me (well, that is what it felt like, all part of the great illusion but it felt so real to me, and I was so very happy to feel like a "family" with someone.)

Steven had been working for a family remodeling their home in Southern Nevada. They bought a second home in Canada and asked Steven if he would remodel their home in Canada as well. We discussed it and I supported him in taking the job because I knew he loved his work and loved this family who had been so good to him. They are a wonderful family, generous and kind. They always treated me like family and included me as Steven and I merged our lives together. I respected them and really liked them and enjoyed our time together. Steven and I made the agreement to not be apart more than two weeks at a time and that sounded wonderful to me. (Little did I know he would have no interest in keeping any agreements.)

It was August 10, 2007 when he moved in. Steven would look at me with love filled eyes and say, "Sheri, I love you, I love 'us' and I am not going anywhere." What seemed to be a blessing at the time was that we lived so well together, we got along so well – mostly because "I don't sweat the small stuff." A few weeks after he moved in I came home one day to find my rather large back yard leveled... it was pulled up... gone! I was so shocked, but Mr. Wonderful assured me by saying, "I want to make a paradise for us." I already knew that Steven does what he wants, and besides, he was paying for it! How wonderful and generous of him. He said, "Dear! I'm not going anywhere!" This backyard was his baby, so I smiled and supported him in his choice. (okay, now here is where we can ask the question: Was he really making the statement, "Yes, I want to be here and this is how I will prove it" or was it part of the "game" to insure he would not get thrown out? Or, did he invest himself into the relationship thinking this would stop the pattern? That is the illusion I wanted to believe.)

Sincerely, this is a man who every morning would awake and turn to me and say, "How wonderful, I get to wake up with a Goddess, every morning without fail!" Steven made me feel so special, you could see the love in his eyes. People used to comment, "He looks as if he could eat you up!" I did not know it at the time but brother they hit the nail on the head.

"I love you so much," he would say, "you are the most amazing woman I have ever met." Every day he would tell me that he felt so blessed to be with me. How could you not love someone so wonderful? He would tease me about it and say "Yep! I came in through the front door." He was proud he had captured his "prize." He even had a "happy dance" he would do when he was especially pleased with himself. It was so charming that we would both laugh out loud.

*(Would it surprise you to know he was secretly following his typical pattern?)*

The first year all was wonderful. In June 2008, I was going to San Diego for the day and somehow my cell phone got wet. Steven told me to take one of his phones and just get a new SIM card. I took one of his three phones and as it was getting dark I stopped at AT&T in Temecula to get a new SIM card. When I got back on the road the phone rang with a text message. I did not really know how to get a text so I just started pushing buttons. Finally the text came up, it said, "Welcome to AT&T," and just below it another text read, "I miss you, when can we play?" Well, you can imagine how my heart just sank as I scrolled to find 133 messages from other women. A few from his ex-wives and too many others to even count. One of the messages was from his third ex-wife, it said, "Oh, Sheri sounds wonderful. I would love to meet her some day." It felt like I was having a falling dream, you know where your heart pounds and you can barely breathe and you wake up just before you hit! I was in shock and tears were welling up the whole way home. I had a 5-hour drive to think about it. Steven called me many times on my way home. Now I know it was probably because he was somewhere doing what he does and wanted a heads up when I was coming back. In my illusion he was missing me and excited for me to be coming home. I didn't know what to do. I thought of confronting him but I knew Steven well enough to know that would bring on his rage, then his brooding, and then the emotional punishing. I decided to say nothing and just see what I could figure out or get a feeling on. I was in an observer mode but when I got home everything seemed just fine. Then, just a week or so later I got a phone bill that I thought was mine (as we have the same phone carrier). I opened it up to find a Canada phone number on it. Hmmm, I thought, he really had no reason to be calling Canada when he was home, so I called the number and it was a woman. What a surprise. I then called Steven to say I was sorry for opening up his bill, but he didn't seem to care, so, apparently he didn't mind my opening the bill.

I began getting the phone bill every month and to my surprise and total shock there were between 60 and 170 phone calls every month to other women. Yes, you read that right 170 calls to other women during a one-month period. It sounds unbelievable but oh so true. I realized that we never had been in the relationship with just us. I now knew that there were six of us in this relationship from the start. There was Jeni, Nana, Verisa, Cheryl, Steven and I! I now knew that much of what Steven was saying to me was just not true. But things seemed to be okay with us, we were getting along so well, he was being the same, wonderful Steven, so, again, I did not confront him. I did, however, ask about his ex-wife Jeni, as there were always at least 30 – 40 calls a month to her and I knew she was now remarried.

Steven said, "Oh, we are just friends and I do know she still loves me, but I don't know what to do about it." I told him that I thought it was not very healthy for either one of them, as it showed a total lack of respect for her new marriage, and was disrespectful, not only to me but also to "us." I also told him I felt it was purely a stroke for his ego to feel that no one could really ever leave him, but I did not want to seem jealous or controlling. I did not feel threatened in any way at this point, and figured he just liked to talk a lot. But as time went on, each month there were more and more numbers from Canada and some women he called four and five times in a day! There were over 30 calls a month from his ex-wife. One month there were 84 texts from a woman in Canada. It was getting really crazy and I wondered how he could even remember my name. Yet he would come home and be the wonderful, loving guy he had always been with me. He was away spending a couple of weeks at a time in Canada and wasn't with me at the opportune time to confront him about it. I missed him every day and it just seemed important to me to make things pleasant and happy when he was home so I just kept putting it off. The weeks and months flew by. Steven was sharing in the expenses of the house and, to be honest, this was also a consideration. It was such a help to have the bills paid for. I was so very much in love and believed this was the Mr. wonderful I had waited for. I wanted that feeling of family so much, even if he was gone some of the time I still felt like part of something special and wonderful. This was my illusion and I was living in it.

### But then things began to change.

He was in Canada the last part of July 08 and beginning of August. He flew home and as he came walking toward me, just off the plane. I could see the love in his eyes was for someone else. He is a master at deception, but I am very, shall we say, energy sensitive and I knew everything had changed. I did confront him in a very soft way. I said, "Your eyes tell me there is someone else."

He said, "NO! you just haven't seen me in awhile. I am just glad to be home with you." He was only going to be home for a week or so and I did not want to have a fight in the first 30 minutes he got off the plane so I just smiled and kept my feelings and hurt inside.

I was not sure until I went to Canada for a month in December 08, when I found two receipts. They were from July earlier that year, and they were both receipts from two different restaurants, just two days apart; each one was for over $300.00. I looked at the dates and it was when Steven was due home in July and had called to say he had to stay a few extra days because of work. One of the receipts was for the night before he came home and the receipt had a time on it of 12:30 a.m., so he had a full evening with whomever and closed the place, and I doubt very much he sent her home… then he comes to me the next day, how is that for a play. I said nothing about seeing the receipts but decided to see if everything Steven was saying was a lie.

When we were in the car going to dinner I said, "Wow, it must feel good to you to not be spending hundreds of dollars on a dinner, because I don't drink!"

He said, "Oh, it has been years since I have done that, not since before I met you." I smiled and did not let him know that I knew he had just once again lied to my face. I kept just observing this behavior, maybe I didn't want to fight and maybe I was just not ready to walk away or have Steven walk away. I would test him to see if he was lying to me. I would say, "Oh, have you talked to Jeni lately?" Or, "How is Nana doing?"

He would say, "I don't know, I haven't spoken to her in a long time." But, I knew he had spoken to her many times just in the previous few days. I had to make some kind of self-defining moments out of all this, and I did feel good about knowing the truth, but amazingly, he would just tell lie after lie after lie. My scientific brain kicked in and I began to be fascinated with this unusual behavior. I had never met a pathological liar before and as long as he did not know what I knew; everything seemed fine to him.

As we moved into the second year, things began to feel a little different, but it would have been easy to explain away due to his travel, had I not known the truth. The long and wonderful conversations became few and far between, his time away in Canada became longer and longer. It was wonderful when I would go and spend weeks in Canada and the trip in December of 08 was for over a month. We had such fun together, going to the local pub and having long and loving dinners at the waterfront restaurants. Yet I knew he had many other female interests and I knew he loved at least one of them. By the time the New Year came the verbal abuse became more and more prevalent. I say abuse because often times I would listen to an hour of how bad I was in business; but he was an expert and yet had no intention or interest in helping me, just criticizing or belittling what I was doing. He began to be more and more nit-picky about everything I did, even what clothes I should wear.

Steven had at least four other girlfriends in Canada that I knew about (not including the prostitute he called every so often or the girl he now employed for the family) and was serious about two other women. When he was home, he was angry, maybe at himself or, maybe he just wanted to be back in Canada. (The phone bills were revealing over 100 calls a month to other women as I stated earlier. It was amazing how one could see by the pattern which woman he would be with on any given night and see the pattern of calls to restaurants, then to his "date." It was unbelievable, all through this Steven was still telling me, "I am the one and he isn't going anywhere." I must have been under some kind of spell to just allow myself to be in this drama and chaos, and know that Steven had brought all this into our wonderful love. He would come home and I just did not want to deal with the brutal side of him. I had seen glimpses of it when he would brood, or not speak to me, and huff around the house like a bully if things weren't exactly like he wanted them. There was no discussion or conversations with feelings other than nothing seemed good enough for him now. Steven was making it clear that I should do more or be more. He no longer seemed to even remember who I was to him and how great we were together. I ask myself now, "Why on earth did I stay in this for so long? Was I just in disbelief? Did I think one day he would wake up and remember us?" Time passed so quickly and before I knew it a year had come and gone with more and more deceit and lies every month.

Steven became more critical and irritated at just about everything. When Steven and I first started dating we took it slow. It was months before he would be spending the night with me. My bedroom was a mess and he had to climb over piles of cloths to be with me. It did not bother him or phase him in the least. He would laugh about it. Now here it was two years later, the bedroom was just about spotless but he would get very upset and critical that there was a box on the floor that had been there for a while. Not a big box, just some papers in a box behind the door. It seemed to be a huge deal now for Steven.

When I would dress up and look exactly the way he wanted me to look, it was like it was in the beginning; he was sweet and nice. But, when I did not dress or look exactly like he wanted, he was distant and brooded, and sometimes made comments like "You're not going out dressed like that are you?" (Dressed in designer jeans and comfortable shoes and a simple top was not what he wanted to see) In his "illusion of me" I was always wearing 5-inch spikes or boots with lots of cleavage showing, perfect makeup, big hair, in a tight fitting suit and jacket at all times. Lets not forget the large hoop earrings! I was now sleeping with my makeup on so I would have that finished look when I awoke. Oh, what a clue! He no longer was telling me how wonderful it was to wake up with a goddess. This caused my heart to sink because I knew he was still saying it, just not to me.

He became angry and threw a fit one evening because my daughter would call and I would answer no matter what time she called. He had separated himself from being a family and that was a harsh blow for me, knowing I was part of that separation. I can not give you a logical reason why I did not confront him, It had been so long for me since I felt like a family with someone, I guess I just didn't want it to be over, despite the lies and cheating and deception.

There were moments he would hold me and kiss me and say, "Sheri, I do love you," and in my mind I would say, "Yes, and about a dozen others as well." Steven continually told me he had never met a woman who captured his imagination the way I did. I believed him because he was still here even in the midst of his sociopathic behavior and knowing that I knew the truth, well some of it anyway.

I was on a mini book tour that took me up through Oregon State. Steven wanted to see me so, I left my car in Portland and flew into Vancouver, Canada. He picked me up and we had a great three days together, then I flew back to Portland while he stayed and "worked." When the phone bill came I saw he had called Erissa, on of his Canadian girlfriends just an hour before I landed. And then he called her again just ten minutes after I got on the plane to come home. It was so disappointing and heart wrenching to know that every day he was making his alliance with other women and lying to me.

Steven loved to BBQ when he was home and have friends over, we both love to entertain. After our friends would leave, he would be on the phone to his girlfriends in Canada. He would go outside so I wouldn't know. Hello… he knew I was getting the phone bill; did he think I wasn't reading it? It was like a bad nightmare. Still his behavior was like a 19-year-old and I just thought it ridiculous, but also dangerous, as he never used condoms in his sexual encounters and I am sure that was true for all his conquests. He was being reckless not only with himself, but he was putting me and the others at risk as well.

The sex was now "just sex" and he liked it rough. (A therapist I had consulted with said this is the way he dealt with his rage.)

There were times he would be wonderful for a few moments, he would really love me (well, I know it wasn't really real, but it felt real and at that moment I was willing to settle for that).

He would hold me tight and say, "Do you feel that? Do you feel me making love to you?"

I would feel like saying, "Well, no. I can feel you pretending to make love with me."

Steven would often pull me close and put me up against the wall in the hall and kiss me passionately. But I noticed that was happening less and less as his interests for others became more and more. It almost felt like the more he wanted to love me the more he wanted to destroy "us" and that would include "me." He worked really hard at it and so as the weeks and months rolled by. I just watched this wonderful connection, this extraordinary love slipping further and further away. I knew him well enough to know he would take any kind of talk about it to be weakness on my part and I knew how he hated any show of weakness in others. I knew by now this would end poorly for me, and so, I just stepped aside and let Steven take his well-rehearsed path. I was heart broken and almost outside myself looking on when he was home. It was so unbelievable for me. I was emotionally battered and spinning from the reality of what I knew had to be the end coming sometime soon.

Steven was now showing much too much of his true colors, sharing bits of his "secret life" with me and I know he was really angry with that as well. He even told me he had broken it off with one of his girls in Canada because she felt they were ready for more like "marriage." It was as if he were trying to bait me into a fight. I did not comply and just shook my head. "As long as he could have the secret life all was well, but to know that I knew was not okay." However, he was sharing his secrets so that I would know certain bits of the truth. I think they call this "crazy making."

One month there were over 25 texts to him in one day from Canada, so I called the number and spoke to a lovely women. I told her I was not angry only seeking some truth and that I noticed she had called my boyfriend over twenty five times in one day! She said, "Who is your boyfriend?" I said, Steven. She said, "OH! Steven, yes, I walk along the pathway in front of his home in Canada and we met and have dated."

I asked, "Did he by any chance mention he has been in a committed relationship and living with someone for two years?" She laughed and said, "NO! He never mentioned it." I said. "Thank you for your time and take care" and hung up the phone. (I asked Steven about the 25 calls in one day and he said, "That's my stalker! I said nothing but wanted to say, "Why was she a stalker? You dated and dumped her and she was angry?) I had now learned that Steven had labeled other women as 'stalkers' as well, apparently women he was in the midst of breaking up with and they weren't understanding his mode of operation, so he refers to them as stalkers. I knew they were most probably confused, angry broken hearted women he had tossed aside but this was his way of not taking responsibility for his actions. He just simply made it seem like their fault and he was the victim.

As I said before, in August of 2008 there were over 84 calls to one woman in one month! And at least eighty more calls to various women, thirteen women in all. Seriously, the phone bill was my saving grace to the truth of what was really going on. I was sinking into a hole and knew I had to find a way to back him away from my heart. It was emotionally debilitating for me. Here I was, doing my best to keep a happy face, remain kind and loving, and all the while living on the memory of what love used to feel like, the warmth and caring now turned to ice and total disregard. I was being totally faithful and honorable and staying in integrity with our agreements, I was alone in this but, still for me, I choose integrity, but now I was so isolated and felt my wonderful feeling of belonging was fading away. Steven would come home and get so angry and accuse me of belonging to "LinkedIn" and insisted this was a dating site. I told him it is a business site, but he just carried on and I wondered how could he even really think that? Accusing me of his behavior was frightening to me and delusionary.

While in Canada, we were visiting some good friends of Steven's, a fine family whose daughter would be getting married the next year. The wife was surprised to meet me and said, "Oh, we had no idea Steven had a girlfriend." (Steven had been working up in Canada for over a year and never even told his best friends about me. They had no idea I even existed.)

I asked, "Has he brought other women over?" She said yes

he had brought other girls over to meet them and they were staying at the "house" where Steven was staying. I was so grateful for her honesty but, I now knew Steven was having serious relationships with many others as I knew he would only bring a serious relation to meet his best friends; he was in full hunting mode.

Steven was now spending more than a month at a time in Canada, and I seemed to be barely a memory for him. When he came home he was short and brutal, buried himself in his work. It was heart breaking for me but I just had to keep a smile on my face, as I knew Steven hated any kind of emotion and saw it as weakness. I felt so grateful for all he had done and so sad that he was such an empty shell. The man/boy who seemed so full of life and was so wonderful to others could not bear to be reminded of the disappointment and the mess he had made and so, it was coming close to his time to move on.

At the end of October 2009, Steven came home for a Halloween party and now I was being treated like a toy and one that did not matter anymore. We came home late from the party and Steven was over the top as far as his alcohol consumption that evening. The bottom line is, he was so rough, throwing me around in the bedroom, my 10$^{th}$ rib was fully fractured and my right arm bone bruised severely. It was crystal clear I was no more than an object to be broken and thrown away, cast off like an old hat, as Steven now had many new games in play and was now in love with at least one of these new flames. Yes, and all the while, he was living with me and telling me he loved me.

There were significant events in early October 2009 and at the end of that October. You will find the details for the last months in the "The Last Straws" section at the bottom of this true story.

November 1, 2009 Steven left for Canada. He would not return to me. On November 13 he was in Canada and he had called one of his local ex gals, the same local ex gal who had the Halloween party. I guess she told Steven that I had said something derogatory about him (which was not true at all), but Steven called me and once again made his alliance with another woman and actually had the nerve to say, " I do not know if I can be with someone who disrespects me." He actually was trying to play the victim and make everything my fault. I was so blown away by it, and I just had enough. I finally stood up for myself and we had a heated conversation about respect. Steven led me to believe he was coming home for the holidays, but that changed.

Three weeks before Christmas, Steven was telling me we would be together having a great vacation in The Bahamas for New Years.

Two weeks before Christmas Steven made the switch; he was now being re-quickened by his 39-year-old girlfriend (and others) in Canada whom he was now "in love" with and so in with the new, (not so new, as he had been dating her for over a year) out with the old. (That would be me, the one he said "I'm not leaving" the one he was creating a paradise for, by tearing up the backyard and the house, leaving holes in the ceiling, wires hanging, gas lines laying on the surface outside and not a hint of feeling any responsibility to finish what he had started.) It was the blizzard for me. After more than 4 years of friendship, including 3 years of relationship, two and a half years living together as "a couple," it was now Christmas; and not a card, a gift, or a thought for the woman he was still saying he loved. The most collateral damage that can be done mentally, emotionally and anyway possible, that is what he did in the typical I love you so I must destroy you, self centered, selfish little boy, I want what I want, I want what I cannot yet have completely, Sociopathic behavior. No wonder some Psychiatrists refer to these people as monsters, pure evil. Really what kind of ice hearted, non feeling, hollow, fake, human must it take to do that two weeks before Christmas? (Hey, there was still the magnetic words on the refrigerator he put together that said, "I am Happy with us.")

I was devastated and angry with myself for feeling so shattered. I was grateful to spend the holidays with my daughter and her family, and they were so wonderful to me. Still, it was incredibly difficult as I was reminded every day that I had no family of my own, the love I thought was real was just a lie, a game, a hunt. Talk about feeling alone and isolated, it was almost too much to bare. I just had to feel as bad as I felt and so started the long process of coming back to me.

On December 30, 2009, Steven was still in Canada. I packed up and moved his clothes and belongings out. About a month went by, Steven came back for a couple of days to go to a convention. We met at a restaurant but he insisted on seeing the house. We came into the house and he looked around, he seemed moved in some way. He saw that he left holes in the wall, and wires hanging and outside leaking pipes. He sat on the couch and cried and said, "I never said I was not in love with you."

I said, "No, but your actions did."

He said, "I am not heartless."

I said, "Your actions say different."

He said, "I have managed to fill my life with short term fixes."

I said, "That is exactly what you wanted." He refused to take responsibility for anything, including my fractured rib and bone bruised arm, but he was excited to show me his new coat.

Steven carries about 17 of the 20 classic traits of a sociopath. Because he knew to stay barely within the bounds of the law and knows exactly what he is doing in his game plan, this puts him in the Social Sociopathic category.

For all you wonderful women out there, if you are not the priority in your man's life, the question is, why would we spend our precious time and waste our life on someone who does not hold us in the same regard we hold them? Get out and get out now. It does not get better and you are too wonderful to be mistreated in any way.

# THE LAST STRAWS WITH STEVEN!
## Straw #1
## Wedding Daze

In early Sept of 2009 there was to be a wedding in Canada. The daughter of a wonderful family and very good friends of Steven's. He was like one of the family and they absolutely adored him. Steven became very good friends with their daughter who was getting married. I believe she is in her late 20s and I know Steven was very fond of her. He got her a position with the family he worked for so they were together a lot of the time. I never thought that there was anything going on between them and I want to believe that, but when he told me he bought her a $500.00 bike as a gift I just had to wonder. I know they were good friends as the phone bills reflected 10 to 20 calls a month outside of work hours. She was very creative and was hired to do some landscape decorating. She did a fabulous job and everyone was happy. Well, almost everyone.

Steven invited me to the wedding and I was so happy to be invited and going back to Canada. He took me shopping at Nordstrom's for a dress, a gown really, and it felt like the good ole days when he would enjoy taking me shopping and watch while I tried on dress after dress. The winner was a beautiful gown, a summer gown, really with beautiful colors of blue and turquoise and of course a plunging neckline. A bit to plunging and so I had them put a hook in front just so

I wouldn't be showing anything inappropriate.

So, off we go to Canada for the wedding. Everyone was there, the owners of the home that is being remodeled and the wonderful neighbors with the creative daughter that is such a great friend of Steven's. The wedding was Saturday, and here it was Thursday evening. We go to the family's home; it is a wonderful heart warming sight. The whole family is they're stuffing envelopes and making centerpieces for the wedding reception. It is an inspiration. Such a wonderful and loving family. The mother of the bride and I sat down on the couch and she was showing me pictures while about 20 feet away Steven and the bride to be are face-to-face in the kitchen, locked in a hug and rocking back and forth, he was stroking her hair in a loving fashion… It looked like something you would expect to see the bride and groom doing, not the bride and my guy. They just stood there in the kitchen with their arms locked around each other, I looked around to see if the groom or anyone else thought it was a bit much but everyone seemed to be smiling, so I did the same.

When we got home (to where we were staying) Steven told me that the bride wanted to go to dinner the night before her wedding, I said great where are we going? "No, she wants to have an intimate dinner with just me," he said.

I replied, "What? Even if I were not standing here do you have any idea how inappropriate that is? No bachelorette party. Just you having an intimate dinner with the bride on the eve of her wedding? What are you thinking?"

"This is a unilateral decision that is common with sociopathic behavior since the only one considered to a sociopath is themselves. Not a thought of how this would effect or cause mental, emotional abuse to his partner or consequences from his choice."

How disrespectful to me and to her groom to be. I felt so invisible, like I did not even exist. Steven got so angry that I could dare to be upset. We had plans for Friday evening and he was just dumping me and taking the bride out? I knew then that I meant nothing, that I was such a hassle for him, because I thought it so wrong. How could he not say to her that my 'significant other' is here with me, the woman I love and have been with for three years is here, why didn't he say we could all go out? I was pushed aside and she became the alpha female, a real eye opener for me. He did not make any provisions for dinner for me or even ask or care what I was going to do. What I wanted to do is get on a plane and never see him again and perhaps that would have been a smart thing for me as the next month and a half was no picnic. Is there anyone out there that feels this was okay? Things would not be the same after this as I knew with certainty that I would be the last one considered, his destruction of our lives together was complete.

# Straw #2
# The Party and Broken Bones

Steven was planning on coming home for Halloween, after all there was a party brewing, It had been almost six weeks he had been gone and now was coming home for four days. When he arrived He worked every minute on the yard at a feverish pace. He put tile down and yelled "FUCK" at me when I stood too close to the edge of a tile. There was really no talking or sharing; he was already somewhere else. I did my best to wear a smile and just appear to be happy. My heart was breaking but I knew if I showed any weakness he would be gone in a flash. (Sociopaths cannot stand emotion around them, they do not tolerate weakness or feelings.) However, we both love the masquerade and of course Steven went in drag as a belly dancer. Wearing my beaded and coined scarves. He looked fabulous and, oh, how he loved the attention. He sat quietly as I put on his make up, his fake eyelashes and dressed him, pinning the scarves and putting his wig on him, he was in attention heaven. Oh, did I mention that the party was at the home of an ex-lover of his?

It was October 31 and Steven was leaving early the next morning to go back to Canada. The party was a blast and Steven drank like there was no tomorrow. Thank God I drove home, boy, was he drunk. When we got home he was extremely rough, throwing me up against the car in a display of sexual dominance. I was being treated like a toy and one he had no regard for at that. We went in and Steven headed for the bedroom, it was late and there was an early flight to catch. Steven was being very rough and rolling around on the bed, pulling me every which way and I was desperately trying to get my scarves off of him before they were torn to shreds. In a flash he twisted me around and jumped on top of me. And crack! I felt my rib in the back go. I was in agony and could hardly breathe.

He said, "Sorry, sorry, sorry" and that was it. There was no way we could be intimate at that point; I was just trying to breathe. He was pissed and turned over and went to sleep. I, of course, lay awake for hours in extreme pain just trying not to move, my whole right side was hot and I was in agony. I was just praying I did not puncture a lung. Oh what a night. At 6 a.m. I took Steven to the airport and barely any words were said. He seemed anxious to be gone.

The truth was he was gone before he ever came home. His hard work destroying what he said he wanted was complete. I knew he had about six or seven girlfriends in Canada and I know he had at least two serious ones, YES, all while he was living with me! He had moved on to the next and I was just a hassle now. Here it is a few weeks from the holidays and I am physically wrecked and broken, although he did call and say he wanted to spend the New Year in the Bahamas with me. He asked me to find some trips so I did. But then came the alliance straw #4.

(By the way my 10th rib was fully fractured in the back and my right arm bone bruised.) It would take over three months to recover and the orthopedic doctor said it would be good for me to have some therapy on the injury. I asked Steven for some funds for the therapy I needed and he said no. He felt no responsibility for it! Gee, what a surprise.

*(On a side note he also just left me high and dry with finances, no discussion no provisions for the woman he was still claiming to love, at the holiday season. I had already spent money on the preparation for our holiday. The rug was pulled out from under me in a flash).*

# Straw #3
# Bathroom Calls

Oh, yes, so here it is November 6, 2009, a Friday evening and Steven is back up in Canada and I am home in the states. Steven usually called me every day (except when he would disappear for a day or two). Anyway, it was 11 p.m. when Steven called and the line was very crackly. He just called for a minute and said, "I will call you in the morning." I said great and good night. The morning comes and no call, all day no call, so at 5:30 p.m. I called him and it goes to voice mail. Then at 7:30 he called and rushed me off the phone with a 40-second call. What is going on? At 11:30 that night (now Saturday night) he called and the line is so crackly again. He told me he went to the Pearl for dinner (a romantic restaurant on the water) then he called me Sunday about 11 a.m. and the line was so bad that I said, "Boy, this line is bad…"

He said, "Oh! I am in the bathroom!" That's how I knew someone was spending the weekend with him and now I was the "other" woman who he hid in the bathroom all weekend to speak to. Then later that evening he called and the line was clear and he was so nice and totally different. Guess he took her home and was now okay to talk to me. Yes, this qualifies as a straw.

# Straw #4
# The Alliance

November 13, 2009, Steven called me about 9:00 p.m. and was very angry. He said, "I don't know if I can be with some one who disrespects me and drags me through the dirt."

I asked, "What are you talking about?"

He said, "I called Nan to thank her for the party (he already knows I know he calls her many times every month) and she said you were talking trash about me."

I said, "So let me get this straight! You call and get false gossip from your ex-buddy with benefits and rather than call me and say, 'Hey, Honey, I heard this'… what's up with that? You just assume that Nan is the virgin queen telling you truths and call me a liar and are upset because I disrespected you? So, you once again chose to make your alliance with another women and just treat me like some spare part! Like I don't even exist?" This was just it for me and we had our first fight in three years. The fight was a doozy and Steven decided to stay with his newer love and family in Canada for the holidays. I did not even receive a card! Two weeks before Christmas he made the switch and was now being quickened by his new games in Canada.

After our heated phone conversation I felt compelled to write him a letter. I was so overwhelmed that after the years of no respect and disregard for me, our relationship and even respect for himself, that Steven could try and turn it around to make himself look like a victim and that I had disrespected him!

# The Last Straw
# Phone Bill Overload

Even though I had been getting the phone bills for over a year and knew that every month there was between 60 and 170 calls to other women. It was amazing and unbelievable to me. But, some how after the month from hell and I got the October 2009 bill it read something like this (keep in mind this is his US phone and Steven also had a Canadian phone he knew I could not see). On this bill there were 70 calls to other women; 14 other women in all. There were three new women, six calls to one and three to the other – two each – 11 texts and calls to another new girl with seven of the calls being in one day. Eleven calls to his favorite; four in one day. (This is a fraction of the calls he usually makes to her so I knew they were spending more and more time together.) There were eight calls to his ex-wife (an all-time low) and nine calls and three texts to the women he left his wife for. So many calls and long conversations that I felt sick and knew I had to save myself from this emotional battering. It was a small straw by comparison, but sometimes it can just be that defining moment that grabs you and causes you to stand up and that this is the moment you say "No More."

## About Steven:

Like the guy in "What Women Want" Really did you see that movie? Well, Steven is like that, his style of capturing hearts is top notch – women flock to him like moths to a flame. We even had waitresses wanting to come home with us when we were out dining. He's the best flirt and makes each person feel that they are the one. He is a gentleman, opening doors and helping with shopping and he is a very hard worker, driven to make all things right. Or so it appears on the outside. He is so wonderful and charming to everyone. This is great unless you happen to be in a "relationship" living with and in what has been said to be a love relationship with him. How crazy was I? Here I was being loving and sexy dedicating myself to our life together and he is dating at least seven other women as if I did not even exist. He has nothing to say about it, doesn't want to discuss it, he is just doing what he does. Just in his game and some how I was invisible, he didn't hear or see or care what he was doing to what we were building, what he continually said he wanted. I once asked if he knew the difference between a lie and the truth and he said yes. So I said, "Are you destroying us deliberately and on purpose?" There was silence but his answer was yes. He was off and running as fast as he could. It is what he has always done only most of his six wives just didn't know it until he left them for the "next one in line." No thought, no care, no guilt or remorse of course not.

Remember the social sociopath only knows how to win and how to vent their rage by destroying that which they love and in so doing fulfills a self-pretending and self-loathing prophecy.

*The person who cares the least has control.*

**The Social Sociopath's Mindset**

# CHAPTER 3

---

# History of
# Sociopathic Behavior

There has always been a very small fraction of society that seems to be beyond the bounds of bad behavior. In the 1830's this disorder was called "moral insanity." By 1900 it was changed to "psychopathic personality." More recently it has been termed "antisocial personality disorder" or Sociopathic behavior. Some critics have complained that, in the attempt to rely only on objective criteria, the parameters have broadened the concept to include too many individuals. The (APD) Antisocial Personality Disorder category includes people who commit illegal, immoral or self-serving acts for a variety of reasons and are not necessarily psychopaths or Sociopaths.

**Under the Umbrella of "Psychopathic:"**
Psychopathy is a personality disorder characterized by an abnormal lack of empathy combined with strongly amoral conduct, masked by an ability to appear outwardly normal. Neither psychopathy, nor the similar concept of sociopathy, is nowadays defined in international diagnostic manuals, which instead describe a category of antisocial/dissocial

personality disorder. However, researcher Robert Hare, whose Hare Psychopathy Checklist is widely used, describes psychopaths as "interspecies predators" as does R.I. Simon. Elsewhere Hare and others write that psychopaths "use charisma, manipulation, intimidation, sexual intercourse and violence to control others and to satisfy their own needs." Hare states that "Lacking in conscience and empathy, they take what they want and do as they please, violating social norms and expectations without guilt or remorse." He previously stated that "What is missing, in other words, are the very qualities that allow a human being to live in social harmony."

# *How did they get this way?*
# Clinical Description

The words in this chapter deserve respect and a careful search of your "loved" one and a careful search of your own heart. Sociopathic behavior does not clear up and go away. It does not change for the better. It progresses further and further down the dark hole until you find the courage to break away or be consumed.

Is this a spoiled child, I want what I want and I want it now behavior? Or, is it emotional detachment from the mother in infancy? Some scientists believe it can be environmental and some say it is in the genes. There is great debate about the scientific data as far as the causes of this detached behavior.

The social sociopath will destroy all who come close, close enough to make them feel; all who step in to "the inner fire" (Later seen in the "Ring of Fire" chapter).

There are two schools of thought; one says there are seven characteristics of a sociopath and another says there are 20 main clinical guidelines as explained in Psychology books, Wikipedia, WebMD. (References can be found in the back of this book. Please note that the Social Sociopath is a term I created to distinguish what I see as two levels of the behavior. The Social Sociopath may "fit in" more easily and some of the traits may be less severe. (Please see in parentheses below.) Up until now there has been no subclassification, only sociopath. I believe there is a distinct line between the purest sociopath and the social sociopath. The social sociopath although carrying the traits and potentially just as volatile has made a life within the bounds of society too most they seem exceptional, the danger and pattern is unleashed on the one or ones closest to him or her.

The agreed upon number one trait is; "The complete unconcern about the adverse consequences for others or self – due to ones actions."

Robert Hare is Emeritus Professor of Psychology, University of British Columbia, where he has taught and conducted research for more than four decades, and President of Darkstone Research Group Ltd., a forensic research and consulting firm. He has devoted most of his academic career to the investigation of psychopathy, its nature, assessment, and implications for mental health and criminal justice. He is the author of several books, including Without Conscience: The Disturbing World of the Psychopaths Among Us, and more than one hundred scientific articles on psychopathy. He is the developer of the Psychopathy Checklist, which follows.

# Dr. Hare's Checklist

*(Sociopathic Traits, Social Sociopathic traits in Italic)*

**1. GLIB and SUPERFICIAL CHARM** – the tendency to be smooth, engaging, charming, slick, and verbally facile. Sociopathic charm is not in the least shy, self-conscious, or afraid to say anything. A sociopath never gets tongue-tied. They have freed themselves from the social conventions about taking turns in talking, for example. *(The Social Sociopath is a master at conversation and seemingly innocent seduction.)*

**2. GRANDIOSE SELF-WORTH** – a grossly inflated view of one's abilities and self-worth, self-assured, opinionated, cocky, a braggart. Sociopaths are arrogant people who believe they are superior human beings. *(The Social Sociopath has learned to direct this cocky attitude and often will make it a point to say, "I have no idea" to even play the underdog as part of his ploy. Still he believes he is a superior human being, and you have just been charmingly invited into his game.)*

**3. NEED FOR STIMULATION or PRONENESS TO BOREDOM** – an excessive need for novel, thrilling, and exciting stimulation, taking chances and doing things that are risky. Sociopaths often have low self-discipline in carrying tasks through to completion because they get bored easily. They fail to work at the same job for any length of time, for example, or to finish tasks that they consider dull or routine. *(The Social Sociopath will often have many risky sexual escapades, or have secret lives going at the same time. This gives him the thrill needed to keep a lid on his sociopathic behavior wile proving to himself over and over how superior he is and how easily he plays others. A pat on his own back, his self serving game goes unnoticed.)*

**4. PATHOLOGICAL LYING** – can be moderate or high; in moderate form, they will be shrewd, crafty, cunning, sly, and clever; in extreme form, they will be deceptive, deceitful, underhanded, unscrupulous, manipulative, and dishonest. "Can create, and get caught up in, a complex belief about their own powers and abilities. Extremely convincing and even able to pass lie detector tests." *(The social sociopath will lie about everything to do with personal relationship. I once asked Steven, "Do you know the difference between the truth and a lie?" He answered yes. I then said, "So you know what you are doing and do it deliberately?" Again the answer was a smile and a yes!)*

**5. CONNING AND MANIPULATIVENESS** – the use of deceit and deception to cheat, con, or defraud others for personal gain; distinguished from Item #4 in the degree to which exploitation and callous ruthlessness is present, as reflected in a lack of concern for the feelings and suffering of one's victims. "They appear to be charming, yet are covertly hostile and domineering, seeing their victim as merely an instrument to be used." *(This is often played out in the social arena where the Social Sociopath will have many games and conquests going at once. He or she may have* *a dozen or more lovers, and confidantes at the same time, lying to each one. When in a "relationship" it can be crazy making as the stories become so fantastic and the lack of concern unbelievable, the behavior goes on regardless of martial status or relationship.)*

**6. LACK OF REMORSE OR GUILT** – a lack of feelings or concern for the losses, pain, and suffering of victims; a tendency to be unconcerned, dispassionate, coldhearted, and un-empathic. This item is usually demonstrated by a disdain for one's victims. "A deep-seated rage, which is split off and repressed, is at their core. Does not see others around them as people, but only as targets and opportunities." *(This behavior is a real heart breaker as you witness your "mate or partner" making choices that let you know, You do not matter, there is no regard and not even a hint of wanting to know how or why you feel the way you feel. The social sociopath is only concerned with his own agenda and his own self gratification and you might as well be a used piece of paper heading for the trash.)*

**7. SHALLOW AFFECT** – emotional poverty or a limited range or depth of feelings; interpersonal coldness in spite of signs of open gregariousness. *(As in #6, this interpersonal coldness is almost too unbelievable to bear, but he or she will think everything is just fine! To the outside world they seem charming, warm and friendly, this is a surface face and only lasts wile the game is in play)*

**8. CALLOUSNESS and LACK OF EMPATHY** – a lack of feelings toward people in general; cold, contemptuous, inconsiderate, and tactless. *(The Social Sociopath can seem to be so concerned, for a moment or so, even demonstrate* *a tear when it suits them, being interested and carrying becomes a tactic for the hunt. The moment he or she falls in love the switch is flipped and they go into high gear with their pattern destroying all they have claimed to want. Destroying the love they have to hate.)*

**9. PARASITIC LIFESTYLE** -— an intentional, manipulative, selfish, and exploitative financial dependence on others as reflected in a lack of motivation, low self-discipline, and inability to begin or complete responsibilities. *(Okay, we know this to be true. But what about the Social Sociopath that is generous, very generous even careless buying gifts and beginning projects when capturing hearts. Pitching in and paying their share of the household? This is a turnaround from the normal pattern but yes it does happen, they may flood you with kindness almost like they are trying to make up for the devastation they know they will leave you with. I for one say thank you and I am grateful for the vision, just not the devastating mess it left.)*

**10. POOR BEHAVIORAL CONTROLS** – expressions of irritability, annoyance, impatience, threats, aggression, and verbal abuse; inadequate control of anger and temper; acting hastily. *(The Social Sociopath has learned to control their anger, they are the first to tell you they cannot tolerate stupidity, and sooner or later the anger and all the above mentioned will start to become more evident. Irritability and annoyance will be a tell-tell sign you are now not the main game, he or she has already left the building. It is important to know when to walk and when to run.)*

**11. PROMISCUOUS SEXUAL BEHAVIOR** – a variety of brief, superficial relations, numerous affairs, and an indiscriminate selection of sexual partners; the maintenance of several relationships at the same time; a history of attempts to sexually coerce others into sexual activity or taking great pride at discussing sexual exploits or conquests. *(This is true in spades! The Social Sociopath is a master but has a flaw, their arrogance can cause them to slip up now and again as they really believe that everyone else is just to dim witted to know what is really going on and after all that is entertainment for the Sociopath. Once they realize you know it is the beginning of the end, as they only want to play with those whom they can take in, those who will look with adoring eyes and believe every word of every lie. Even if you accept the insane behavior the thrill for them is gone for they have been found out and what fun is that?)*

**12. EARLY BEHAVIOR PROBLEMS** – a variety of behaviors prior to age 13, including lying, theft, cheating, vandalism, bullying, sexual activity, fire-setting, glue-sniffing, alcohol use, and running away from home. *(Knowing someone's past is as important as knowing someone's present, do your homework or pay the price.)*

**13. LACK OF REALISTIC, LONG-TERM GOALS** – an inability or persistent failure to develop and execute long-term plans and goals; a nomadic existence, aimless, lacking direction in life. *(The social sociopath may have some good goals that seem well within reach. They may be the head of their own company or business. They may be well respected in a chosen field. However they seldom finish jobs or assignments, failure to complete what they start. In there personal life they are nomadic, going from one to another with lack of direction, driven by addiction to sex, alcohol,* *and the game, seeking the party life with out responsibility or care, intense and driven. Let it be noted that not all social sociopaths are alcoholic, some may not drink at all, but all have an intense sexual drive or addiction.)*

**14. IMPULSIVITY** – the occurrence of behaviors that are unpremeditated and lack reflection or planning; inability to resist temptation, frustrations, and urges; a lack of deliberation without considering the consequences; foolhardy, rash, unpredictable, erratic, and reckless. *(I would have to put a star on inability to resist temptation, reckless and uncontrollable urges and of course not a thought of consequences for self or others, a life based on reckless behavior)*

**15. IRRESPONSIBILITY** – repeated failure to fulfill or honor obligations and commitments; such as not paying bills, defaulting on loans, performing sloppy work, being absent or late to work, failing to honor contractual agreements. *(The Social Sociopath may be great at work, even be a perfectionist, but in their personal life they do not complete anything, they certainly do not honor agreements especially ones made with a partner. They demand and expect you to honor agreement but alas they are exempt from any such bounds.)*

**16. FAILURE TO ACCEPT RESPONSIBILITY FOR OWN ACTIONS** – a failure to accept responsibility for one's actions reflected in low conscientiousness, an absence of dutifulness, antagonistic manipulation, denial of responsibility, and an effort to manipulate others through this denial. *(This trait is true in spades, somehow they will make* *it your fault, Twist it all around and what is scary is they actually may really believe it. They may have had dozens of affairs, been emotionally and verbally abusive, demanding and demeaning but they will leave telling you the bedroom was messy and they just can not get past that.)*

**17. MANY SHORT-TERM MARITAL RELATIONSHIPS** – a lack of commitment to a long-term relationship reflected in inconsistent, undependable, and unreliable commitments in life, including marital. *(Hang a big star on #17. Even if there is a long term marriage or two the pattern does not stop. The only thing consistent about a Social Sociopath is their inconsistency, they only commit and care about their own immediate gratification and to win the game, Hey, if they have to lie or be kind or seem patient to get what they want so be it.)*

**18. JUVENILE DELINQUENCY** – behavior problems between the ages of 13 through 18; mostly behaviors that are crimes or clearly involve aspects of antagonism, exploitation, aggression, manipulation, or a callous, ruthless tough-mindedness. *(If they are lucky someone in their life will help them to see that the law will win. It is at that point many choose to stay within the bounds of society, barley but non the less they choose the road of the Social Sociopath.)*

**19. REVOCATION OF CONDITIONAL RELEASE** – a revocation of probation or other conditional release due to technical violations, such as carelessness, low deliberation, or failing to appear. *(Some matters are just not that interesting or important to them. For those who did not have a caring person to guide them at the critical moment this trait will be more severe and cause run ins with the law.)*

**20. CRIMINAL VERSATILITY** – a diversity of types of criminal offenses, regardless if the person has been arrested or convicted for them; taking great pride at getting away with crimes. *(The Social Sociopath may like to drink and drive, forget to pay tickets and have a lack of regard for most rules, however they would just as soon use their talents on hunting and conquering hearts as it is more physically rewarding, easier and there is no law against breaking hearts and homes, no law against lies and deception, this is a big green light for the Social Predator. Just having a great time and party, party, party, they thrive on "getting away with it.")*

# Other Related Qualities:

*Contemptuous of those who seek to understand them* – Social Sociopaths do not like to be questioned about what or why they are doing anything. They will flee at the attempt of someone wanting to understand them. That would be way to revealing. They do not want to be understood, just obeyed.

*Does not perceive that anything is wrong with them* – Hey, they are superior so any flaws must be with you. They will always rationalize by making it your fault. Somehow, they seem to look like the good guy and people will think what the heck happened? So and so must have really done something terrible for this wonderful charming guy to have left.

*Authoritarian* – This may include controlling behaviors including punishing you emotionally, mentally or for some even physically if they do not get their way. Brooding, withholding, and all kinds of tantrums including the silent treatment. This is controlling behavior at its finest.

*Reacts to imaginary situations* – "He anticipates betrayal, humiliation or punishment. He imagines rejection and rejects first to 'get it over with.' He will harass to get your reaction and try to make you look out of control.

*Unpredictable* – in marriage or a relationship they can go from nice to dangerous in a split second, become vengeful and often behave like Dr. Jykel and Mr. Hyde. Sharp mood swings might be an understatement.

Secretive.

Conventional appearance.

Has an emotional need to justify their crimes and therefore need their victim's affirmation (respect, gratitude and love).

Ultimate goal is the creation of a willing victim.

Incapable of real human attachment to another.

*NOTE: The severity of these traits may vary.*

(The above traits are based on the psychopathy checklists of H. Cleckley and R. Hare.)

Social Sociopath's are usually highly intelligent and have learned the motions of love. Holding hands, opening doors, a master of conversation they allow you to feel so bonded, so accepted and included, they seem to be caring and understanding as long as you keep the story short. Remember, they lose interest quickly and have no room for errors or explanations. If you repeat yourself or ask a question they may look at you as if you were some inferior life form. They will often openly express how they loathe stupidity. Once you become a bit closer you are privy to how they may really feel, underneath the charisma and charm, calling others idiots or incompetent. (Only when they are alone with you, so no one else hears.) Their cheery compliments fade to negative disgust for others.

I remember one day when driving, a car passed us. Steven was in a "mood" and he yelled, "I wish you a horrible life, you idiot! I wish ill for you and your family!" He turned to me and said, "What an idiot, I mean it, I hope they all have a horrible life!" It was said with such anger and passion that I was horrified! Where did that come from? I looked at him and shook my head, but I smiled and said nothing.

Inside I was looking at him saying to myself, "What happened to Steven? Where is the wonderful gentle human I met and fell in love with? What kind of pain must he be in to lash out so?" But, then I woke up and told myself to stop it! He has always been this way, just hiding it while he was hunting me, and knows exactly what he is doing and saying. The rage was beginning to bubble up and beginning to show more. This is usually their cue to begin the final phase of their pattern, as they are well aware that they are "showing."

In the beginning they are so thoughtful and pleasant. There will be no signs of disrespect or disregard. Steven was so patient and kind it was amazing. Their talent for good conversation is unmatched unless you have been around long enough to see the same words and conversation come in calculated different areas of interest. You may notice that the male sociopath may speak, suggest, or blurt out totally inappropriate sexual requests at times. This trait will most probably not come out until you are in the ring of fire*. Yes, he is still-hunting, still being charming and inviting to all.

Is there a difference between someone who is Narcissitic and someone who is sociopathic?

According to Hare, many psychopaths are glib and superficially charming, and can be excellent mimics of normal human emotion; some psychopaths can blend in, undetected, in a variety of surroundings, including corporate environments. According to some, there is neither a cure nor any effective treatment for this disorder; there are few medications that can instill empathy, while psychopaths who undergo traditional talk therapy only become more adept at manipulating others. However, other researchers suggest that psychopaths may benefit as much as others from psychological treatment, at least in terms of effect on behavior. According to Hare, the consensus among researchers in this area is that psychopathy stems from a specific neurological disorder, which is biological in origin and present from birth although this was not what was reported by a 2008 review, which instead indicated multiple causes and variation between individuals. It has been estimated by some, that less than one percent of the general population are psychopaths.

When trying to understand the difference (if any) between narcissists and sociopaths, it is important to understand why we have psychiatric diagnoses in the first place. We have diagnostic categories because people go to professionals seeking help for their emotional/psychological issues. The problem is that people who are grandiose, exploit others, lack empathy, and apparently have no conscience are unlikely to seek mental health treatment. Therefore, people with these symptoms are poorly understood. This is also the basic reason why this set of symptoms has been labeled both narcissism and sociopathic.

To further the confusion for victims of what is sometimes called "love fraud." The psychologist, Dr. Million, has described the amorous narcissist. "Such people are charming, articulate, charismatic and emotionally exploitative of their lovers. The amorous narcissist, like Don Juan, seeks conquest in his relationships." Below is the best example of an amorous narcissist I have seen, yet she (correctly) calls him a sociopath:

I was completely taken in by a sociopath over a year ago. I had never met anyone who was so attentive, charming, complimentary, good looking… oh, the list goes on. I felt I had not only met Mr. Right, but Mr. Perfect. This was a very cultured and well-educated man. Unlike the stereotypical sociopath, he holds a good job -can even be considered a "captain of industry." We live in different cities, so it was even easier for him to fool me. He would call me two to three times a day – send text messages, write e-mails. I wondered sometimes how he got the time to do all this. But it was almost impossible for ME to get him on the phone. He said he was at a meeting, at a business dinner, etc.

He also seemed to not have many good friends. And all the people he mentioned were women – someone who went to the symphony with him – and had for a long time, someone who was a biking partner, etc. He said his friendships with these people were built around common interests, which I thought was fair enough. After six months and visits back and forth, his romantic spiel was not as effusive, which I thought normal. I also began noticing a lot of inconsistencies and lies. I caught him in a lie about where he was – he said he was in one city on work and it turned out that he was in another city on vacation – and I knew it had to be with another woman! Anyway, I expressed my distrust and he accused me of being suspicious for no reason. He said I had a mental illness and should have my head examined. I got so blisteringly angry when he said this that I told him that I would prove to him that my suspicions were warranted. I embarked on a detective spree and uncovered four women who he was courting the same way. One was the official girlfriend in the city where he lived. The others were mistress-type girlfriends. I spoke with all of them. And then I presented him with the evidence. He did not have much to say other than that he had "done everything for me, shown me a good time, bought me gifts…" and did not know why I was upset. I know now that there are others. It is like he needs to get all the women he meets to fall in love with him. (From, Ask Dr Leedum*.)

I think that sociopaths and narcissists are very different, although they both demonstrate a certain amount of "narcissism," which is confusing terminology for some people. There is clinical "narcissism" the disorder, and narcissism the trait of self-love, overconfidence, delusions of grandeur, etc. "Narcissism" the disorder is just a term for a bundle of traits that happens to include narcissism

73

the trait. Narcissism isn't necessarily the dominant trait of the narcissist, although it is certainly a prominent one. Sociopaths also frequently manifest the narcissistic trait, but the sociopath would believe he has more justification for his narcissism, and with good reason. The sociopath is exceptional -- his brain is hardwired differently to think rationally all the time, to exploit, to be a predator/scavenger. I don't think this is true of narcissists. I believe narcissism is deeply based in self-deception. As Fyodor Dostoevsky said in The Brothers Karamazov: A man who lies to himself, and believes his own lies, becomes unable to recognize truth, either in himself or in anyone else, and he ends up losing respect for himself and for others. When he has no respect for anyone, he can no longer love, and in him, he yields to his impulses, indulges in the lowest form of pleasure, and behaves in the end like an animal in satisfying his vices."

# CHAPTER 4

---

# Accompanying Behaviors, Disorders and Additions

*(There were many sources and resources in this discovery process. You will find the details in the glossary at the back of the book.)*

**This is a ball of fun rolled into one:** Narcissistic, sexual addiction along with alcohol addiction or abuse, pathological lying and general disregard for family or partners. These traits are varying and not easy to pick out when in a social atmosphere. In the up coming story, Katherine's husband Anthony, did not even drink and we find varying degrees of certain behaviors. When in a close relationship these traits become shinning stars on a daily basis, a way of life for the carrier and eventually devastating to the one on whom they have been focused on or to whom they have expressed "words of love." If you get close enough, that feeling comes from the Social Sociopath so rises all the rage that has been pushed down. They will loathe you for "making them begin to feel." The hunt will be over and they will be on to the next whom they have been grooming for the position for months maybe even years. The sociopath must run or be exposed. Having multiple games going at once is how they keep the syndrome at bay; feeling like they are loved and looked up to is a must. Feeling like they are in control is important for them although, they do not realize just how out of control they are, or do they?

Although, these traits usually lurk beneath the surface of the charming and lovable social sociopath, the behavior and items listed in this chapter may be a way for you to be able to define or at least recognize what is happening. The social sociopath usually has a combination of sex, verbal abuse, alcohol, and a fairy tale quality to the way they view life. Sociopaths almost always love to party, they will be the charming storyteller at the bar, disguised as a heavy social drinker, it adds to their persona as being care free and engaging. Narcissistic and reckless they will risk their own safety, as well as yours, with sexual encounters and unprotected, of course.

"They might not realize that they have a drinking problem. They might not drink every day, might not drink large amounts when they drink. They might go for days or weeks between drinking episodes. They might say they are a "social drinker." So says WebMD." On the flip side they may choose not to drink at all.

What is a "social drinker"? A social drinker is discussed clinically as a person who has a drink or two while socializing and the emphasis is on "social." Most people might socialize two or three nights a week. Or, some households have a "Happy Hour" with friends and family. So, how many drinks does it take to abuse alcohol?

A true alcoholic actually doesn't require many drinks because the blood alcohol level remains high from drinking every day. If you go to a party, a pub, restaurant, on a date, or at a friend's home, have a drink before dinner and one or two during or after would be considered social. When three to five drinks are consumed daily before or during dinner that would be considered more than social. So when you are in the company of someone who has three or four before and during dinner and then another three to six or more after dinner, we would consider that abusing alcoholic. Even worse, this person could be in total denial. The Social Sociopath may do his best work when a bit tipsy. Denial is part of the game as the sociopath under the smooth surface is arrogant and feels superior to everyone else. Leveling the playing field by his being drunk is stimulating to him and may add to his "high" of the conquest.

Sexual addiction is a whole and an interesting subject unto itself. This is the area that can define whether you are dealing with someone who is just self-centered and self-absorbed, a malignant narcissist, or are you dealing with a true-life social sociopath?

CNN described it as: Sex Addiction, also called compulsive sexual behavior, is like a gambling compulsion or alcoholism: It's about devoting your free time to a behavior that you cannot stop, even if you damage relationships or prompt other negative consequences. That could mean extensively using pornography, having affairs, sleeping with prostitutes, and masturbating excessively, to the point where such behaviors get out of control.

What causes sexual addiction anyway? Sexual addiction is usually a result of sexual abuse in childhood. Although there may be other psychological and emotional reasons.

A counseling center in Colorado states it like this: "The biological addict is someone who has conditioned their body to receive endorphins and enkephlines (brain chemicals) primarily through reinforcing a fantasy state with the ejaculation that provides these chemicals to their brain. Psychologically, the need to medicate or escape physical, emotional or sexual abuse can demand a substance, the early addict finds the sex medicine usually before alcohol or drugs.

Spiritually, a person is filling up the God hole in them with their sexual addiction. The addiction is their spirituality; it comforts them, celebrates them and is always available and present. Then there is the sex addict who can be two or even three of the above reasons. This is why a specialist in sex addiction is the best route for recovery with sex addiction."

### *Yes, a sex addict is a drug addict and here is why:*
When we are aroused our brain releases chemicals that give us that "high" that euphoric feeling that all is right with the world. Those moments of ecstasy flood our systems with these chemicals and it feels wonderful. A sex addict needs a "fix" just like a drug addict and paralleled with a drug addict is also the fact that the planning of obtaining the drug can be more satisfying than the act of doing the drug. The sex addict is driven to be in a constant state of "planning;" it is what gets him high. This is much of what motivates the social sociopath.

**\*Below are eleven question asked by sexhelp.com**

1. Were you sexually abused as a child or adolescent?
2. Did your parents have trouble with sexual behavior?
3. Do you often find yourself preoccupied with sexual thoughts?
4. Do you feel that your sexual behavior is not normal?
5. Do you ever feel bad about your sexual behavior?
6. Has your sexual behavior ever created problems for you and your family?
7. Has anyone been hurt emotionally because of your sexual behavior?
8. Are any of your sexual activities against the law?
9. Have you made efforts to quit a type of sexual activity and failed?
10. Do you feel controlled by your sexual desire?
11. Have important parts of your life (such as job, family, friends, leisure activities) been neglected because you were spending too much time on sex or thoughts of sex?

Medicine.net describes it like this: The term "sexual addiction" is used to describe the behavior of a person who has an unusually intense sex drive or an obsession with sex. Sex and the thought of sex tend to dominate the sex addict's thinking, making it difficult to work or engage in healthy personal relationships.

Sex addicts engage in distorted thinking, often rationalizing and justifying their behavior and blaming others for problems. They generally deny they have a problem and make excuses for their actions.

Sexual addiction also is associated with risk-taking. A person with a sex addiction engages in various forms of sexual activity, despite the potential for negative and/ or dangerous consequences. In addition to damaging the addict's relationships and interfering with his or her work and social life, a sexual addiction also puts the person at risk for emotional and physical injury.)

We all hear of infidelity in a relationship and many have experienced it. For most people it is a fling, or a one night of "it just happened" and unfortunately for many it may be a long-term affair. Most men or woman will usually come clean and be truthful if you asked them. That is, if you are significant in their life and they do not want to lose the relationship they are having with you. Their alliance will be with you.

The Social Sociopath is in his or her own realm, they will lie and deceive you for as long as possible, It most likely will not be one single affair but many, many affairs. Some may be for an hour or two, for a night, some will be for a week or a month and some will be for months and years. The thrill of "getting away with it" is a strong pull for this social predator and in many cases this is how they will be able to release their rage a little bit at a time. They have a need to feel plugged in and how better than to really be "plugged in." This allows them to feel for a moment they are normal and can feel, but as the minutes go by and the euphoria wears thin they will be done and gone, on to the next. In their fairy tale world they are helping everyone, seeing themselves as a modern day Robin Hood. They give and they give not even seeing the truth of the web of lies and deceit they weave. They are the hero in their own minds and the flip side of that is they also know they are the villain, the one who brings the disappointment and devastation, after all, someone has to pay for their pain and feeling of separation and so, they plunge in and it's a big world out there. The Social Sociopath knows exactly what they are doing. Their encounters are carefully set up and carried out. What begins as a chance meeting very quickly turns into another game for them. How long will it take for this one to fall? How long until I walk away and am done? They know every move and know they are leaving a trail of bewildered and broken hearted women (or men) but that does not phase them because they are fully justified in their minds and since they are emotionally detached, feelings play no part in this game and they are not capable of truly feelings for anyone but themselves.

# In Plain English

You can like, love or like, hate, pity, or envy a social sociopath it is all up to you because, it matters not to the person who is wearing and going through his (or her) life as a social predator, a "Social Sociopath."

To love a sociopath is to love an illusion. It is living in the illusion of love. A sociopath is incapable of emotional attachment so the normal boundaries we place on our selves to remain in truth and integrity with others just do not apply. It's not like they are breaking any of their rules because they do not have any. Only as it applies to achieving their goals, getting what they want, and what they want is a good hunt with a brief time of re quickening. "To win the game."

To us, this re-quickening looks and feels like love, love is a feeling, state of being and requires emotional attachment. It requires the wearer to have a conscience, a sense of moral ethics and the ability to be truthful, respectful and forthright with another human being. Please know, a social sociopath does not have this ability. Remember, we are talking about a personal involvement.

In the workplace they can be loyal or appear loyal, be a genius at what they do. So charming and charismatic, usually everyone just loves them. They are self-starters, persuasive and highly skilled in their chosen field. As long as no one pushes them or crosses them, all is well. Often they are workaholics; as being king of there own realm at work can be far easier than hunting. But, hunt they will and hunt they must. (Besides if everyone thinks they are working all the time, this is a perfect cover for their secret life.)

Some sociopaths are the opposite of this and act out this disorder in an opposite way in the workplace. They just want to party and have a good time. They may seem lazy or unable to focus on just one job. They will go through jobs, friends and expect the one closest to take care of them; they will have a sense of entitlement, their own entitlement.

Most who carry this trait are great at starting projects, but they are famous for not finishing anything. A wise man said, "You can define a man's character by how he finishes a project, not by how he begins it."

For the 96% of us who have true feelings, have strived all of our lives to be the best person we can be, to honor and respect all life around us and cherish our loved ones and our friends this seems unthinkable and unbelievable. Please know these are facts, and the truth. You have free will to embrace whomever you like. I ask that you read the chapter "Ring of Fire" very carefully, take it to heart, and know it is true and coming from someone who has lived it, been taken in by it, believed in it, loved it and fell in love with it, awoke from the illusion of it, studied it, learned it, been bewildered by it, felt it leaving, grieved it, been grateful for it and finally let it go.

"*I am the worlds most dangerous predator*

*Everything about me invites you in*

*My face, my voice, my smell*

*I invite you in for the kill*"

from Twilight, the movie

# CHAPTER 5

---

# Case Study # 2:
# "I Put a Spell on You"

My name is Katherine, and it was 25 years ago, when I first met my now ex-husband, Anthony. Looking back there may have been some red flags but in the moment everything seemed fine and wonderful.

I met Anthony when I was 19 years old, he was 24 … Italian, good looking, and an entertainer. He was very outgoing, great personality, a take-charge kind of guy, loved family, and lived to entertain and socialize. Anthony was a charmer, he hugged and kissed everyone, young and old. His affection to people was overwhelming, he bear-hugged the men, flirted and complimented the women, played with the kids, told jokes, and raved about his wife … me. What or who could be better? We were married after 5 years of living together and 16 years later, we had a beautiful baby girl.

Life revolved around our family, and when I say family I mean, my parents, sister, brother-in-law, Anthony, myself, our daughter Nikki. Our family was so close that it was almost unreal. Anthony loved to cook so we had Sunday dinners every week at our house (our family plus 10 to 12 friends, dinner was always for 16 or more). Our "friends" came and went as if through a revolving door. Anthony would be the best friend anyone would want, and in time, something would happen and the friendships ended. But, it was usually because he met so many people on a daily basis that we could only invite so many for dinner. So, our guests were a constant turnover.

The family would meet for lunches and breakfast during the week, we'd go to movies three to four times a month, take vacations together, and the holidays... well they were spectacular, surrounded by family and 20+ friends every time. Sounds great doesn't it? Well, it was ... most of the time. You may be thinking, "Gee, that doesn't sound bad at all, what is she talking about?" As I mentioned, I can not write all that happened during those 25 years (that may be another book all together), but the red flags and warning signs were there at every turn; I just didn't see them.

I loved my husband, I stood by him and defended him for 25 years in the way he acted, the things he did or said, the (many) legal problems he got into ... because, it was never his fault ... he was the victim ... it was always someone else's fault... or people were jealous of him (according to Anthony). I believed him, the family believed him, and so we bought it ... lock, stock, and barrel. Someone once told me that I was under a spell with Anthony. I thought they were crazy ... until I divorced him and was away from him for about eight months, and then it hit me ... I was! I was under a spell, living in an illusion. But, then again, so was my entire family.

Life with Anthony was a roller-coaster ride to say the least.

I have come to realize that Anthony was a full-fledged "Social Sociopath" and the havoc he wreaked on all of us was devastating.

## I'll start my story with just the last few years of my marriage.

So, here we are, married about 22 years. My daughter, Nikki is eight years old, and Anthony has been selling cars (out of our house) for over a year. Some of the career choices he's made over the years have all fallen apart. (None of course, were his fault) so he decided to do something from home. But (seriously) Anthony was the absolute best salesman ever; he could sell snowballs to Eskimos! And so, he started buying and selling cars, and making quite a bit of money. I did NOT want him doing this out of the house (it's illegal to sell cars without a license), but of course, I don't know what I'm talking about. Long story short, Anthony sells a car to an uncover cop, the police raid our home, arrest Anthony, there's a court case, Anthony is put on probation and has to pay back "swindled" customers, (those good deals on low mileage cars... were because he rolled the odometers back!). Anthony told the judge that he got the cars that way (all 200 of them) and, of course, it wasn't his fault ... again. He got two years' probation.

Over 25 years of marriage, Anthony had sporadically gotten into trouble, but managed to talk his way out of everything. We believed him when he told his stories, in great detail, and how he was attacked, or victimized, or in the wrong place at the wrong time. He just seemed to be unlucky most of the time, or misunderstood. He talked his way out of things with police, judges, lawyers, everyone. But, it never seemed so bad that would give me cause to divorce him. The bigger incidents were spread out over the years, so they didn't seem to be a pattern … and what kind of wife would I be if I divorced this man because someone attacked him, or just because he didn't pay his tickets? I thought that everyone has faults … I shouldn't be too hard on him.

Sociopaths win your sympathy and devotion. He can convince you that he has been misunderstood all of his life, unfortunate things just happen to him, and you are the only one that understands him.

Anthony created chaos within his life, employment, careers, money, sex life, parenting, everything. I spent 25 years making excuses for him, on edge at what he might say or do, and I never noticed that there was a big or even bigger problem … it was Anthony, not the circumstances. Even though he was the family guy, and loved to throw parties, he was also very controlling. Everything had to be about him, he had to be the center of attention, his ego was huge, and everything was about his career, his goals, his likes, dislikes, it was all about him.

Others viewed him as being cocky, he saw himself as being secure. It was shortly after the car-selling episode that my parents, Anthony, and me started a magazine. I was the editor and Anthony was in charge of sales (of course). Anthony didn't want anything to do with the magazine, (as it wasn't his, it was mine) and we had to beg him to come help with getting sales for the publication. So, after a few months of us begging him to help out, he came on board.

The magazine was doing well, and we were invited to cover an exclusive party; that's when we met Roberta and Mel Connor. They were lovely people and we soon became best friends. They became part of the family and every Sunday we got together. This included Roberta, Mel, their daughter Christie – 14 years old, and son Tyler - six years old, along with 10 to12 additional friends. The Connors also became part of the weekly lunches, breakfasts, movies, and trips and even the holidays.

I had not had a best friend in about 20 years. Anthony and I had an abundance of friends, but they were all people Anthony would meet and invite to dinner. And those "friends" came and went; like going through a revolving door. The few girl friends I had when we first met, just sort of went away … they either didn't like Anthony, or Anthony would let me know that they weren't true friends … and before I knew it, they were gone. So we had "our" friends that would come over. Roberta and I hit it off; it was wonderful to have such a good friend again.

Roberta's daughter, Christie was a sweet girl, and she would babysit my daughter quite often. Christie was rather a large girl for her age, she was about 5'10", 180 pounds, and her bras had to be specially made (46DDD). She looked about 23, but the reality was she was only 14. Christie was a straight-A student, and so was her brother, Tyler. Roberta and her family went to church every Sunday. Anthony, an Italian-Catholic, went to church every Sunday also, but he stopped going to full Mass years ago. He would go in to say a prayer, light candles, and receive communion only. Our house had a statue of Mary, one of Jesus, the rosary – and

crosses on the wall. A typical Italian home, you might say.
During this year, we had many parties and celebrated many
occasions, one being Christie's 15th birthday. She was now
getting to the age where she wanted to get a learner's permit.
Her stepfather Mel was an inpatient guy, very quiet, and
short-tempered; Christie wanted to learn how to drive and
Mel didn't want much to do with it. Anthony offered to teach
her how to drive after school. He had more freedom to leave
the magazine. I however, was there from early morning to
late at night. Roberta thought it would be a good learning
experience for Christie to work at the magazine, it seemed
perfect; Anthony would pick Christie up after school, give
her some driving lessons, and bring her to the office to work.
The drive from school and to home made for some nice
"driving lesson" time. Everyone wins!

Anthony was very affectionate with everyone. And, with
our family as close as it is, hugs, kisses and mass amounts
of affection are given on daily basis. You may wonder if
I ever got jealous if Anthony was flirtatious or affectionate
with other women. The answer is, yes, I did! Anthony was
an entertainer and there were always groupies, I watched
closely and was on high alert and did not see how being in
the entertainment business was cause for such heavy flirting.
I was wary and at times mistrusting.

Anthony was very persistent, and assured me that it was part
of the entertainment business, part of being Italian, that he
just loves people. He told me that he only fell in love once,
and that was with me, and he would never cheat on me.
Anthony made sure he always gave the highest compliments,
and praises to me in front of everyone. And, he was always

telling people, "my wife is the best, I couldn't do it without my wife" and so on. So, over the years, I became more secure and less jealous than I was at 20. But still, I had one eye on the women and one on him … I would listen to what he was telling me and believe it.

As with all families, there are ups and downs and problems from time to time. So, when Christie started telling my family and I that her stepfather Mel is a cold person, and yells at her, and that Roberta is too strict, and that she likes it at our house better, we listened and explained how parents have their own way of raising their children. Christie was now 15, a teenager and with that comes a whole new set of challenges for parents. So, it seemed perfectly normal for her to express her feelings about what she saw as problems at home. Anthony was still picking her up at school and teaching her to drive. She was thrilled about that and was confiding in Anthony about her personal challenges. Roberta thought it was good that Anthony could talk to her.

One day, Anthony was at our office, and got a call from a Detective Johnson. The detective asked Anthony if he could come down to the station and answer some questions. Anthony said he was extremely busy and couldn't and asked what this was regarding. Johnson said that he had received an anonymous phone call from a girl at Chilton High School stating that he and Christie were "dating." Anthony explained that he is like family to Christie, and is picking her up at school and teaching her to drive, he said there is no "dating." The detective insisted that Anthony come down there, but Anthony refused and got extremely angry over the accusation, and hung up. He immediately called Mel and

Roberta. They informed us that they knew about this, but had told the detective to disregard it, as it was ridiculous and they knew the phone call was from Christie's ex-girlfriend, and she was trying to cause problems.

A week after that, I got a call from Roberta saying Christie had run away. I received a call shortly after that, from my sister; Christie had run away and gone to her house, which was closer than ours. She wanted to come to our house, so my sister and brother-in-law brought her over. Christie was crying and hysterical, saying that she couldn't go back, it was horrible there, and wanted to stay with us. We calmed her down, and called Roberta and Mel to come over. Both families explained that she can't live with us, and she needed to go home. Roberta and Mel told Christie that they would do whatever was needed, including counseling, to fix things and make it right.

There was a lot of drama going on with Christie; her grades were dropping, she was having problems with her ex-girlfriend, she was having control issues with her parents, and various other teenage problems. When she would come to work at the magazine, she would spend most of her time talking and crying to Anthony about her problems.

We were all concerned about Christie; it's hard dealing with teenagers and to hear how she hated her parents was very difficult for me, as we were such good friends. Anthony was just great with her, listening to her, giving her advice, teaching her to drive, and we thought it was great that she had a father figure to confide in, at least someone to talk to. One morning, Anthony decided that it would be best if

Christie didn't work at the magazine anymore, and said she should go home and work at her family relationship. He hugged her and said how sorry he was, but that she would be getting her driver's license next year and would have more freedom, and could come over any time she wanted. Christie was broken hearted, crying, and sobbing; Roberta came to pick her up.

## REALITY HITS

Ten days after Anthony let Christie go at the magazine, my secretary came into my office and anxiously said "Katherine, there are four FBI agents in Anthony's office!" As I walked into his office, my 8-year-old daughter, along with my entire staff was watching. I asked the FBI agent what was going on, and he replied, "We're arresting him on 26 counts of Statutory Sexual Assault of a Minor, Christie Connor." Anthony was handcuffed, and saying it was all a lie, it never happened, and to call his attorney.

They took him away, I called my parents, and Roberta (but she said she was instructed not to talk to me) and I called our attorney, John (who was a family friend). I couldn't believe it! Could this really be happening? What is going on?

Anthony insisted that it was all a lie; he would never do such a thing, that he loved Roberta and Mel with all his heart and would never do such a thing; she was a child for God's sake!

The next few days were a nightmare! The police came to my office and confiscated everything in Anthony's office (his computer, files, notes, etc.). Then they came to my home with a search warrant, and went through everything, in every room, taking all sorts of things and even my computer. The whole thing was embarrassing, humiliating and devastating to say the say the least.

In the meantime, our attorney was taking statements, Anthony was calling from jail every 30 minutes, angry that he was there, as he had not done anything wrong, he was innocent, and was going to sue the police department for false arrest, and breaking into tears constantly saying, "How could the Connors have allowed something like this to happen; we were like family!!" And he would cry and say how hurt he was that anyone would even consider him doing something like this. He wanted out of jail, for bail to be posted. "Get me out of here. I'm innocent!" It was a traumatic, and nerve-wracking week for everyone as you can well imagine.

I was at my parent's house, when our attorney John came over to give me a copy of Christie's deposition. I sat down to read the 300-page document, and as I read, the cold rush of fear and anger swept through me ... I knew she was telling the truth. Anthony had lied about so many things that had taken place over the past year and a half, it was frightening. He had been having sex with Christie for about a year! Detailed accounts of places, events, times, things that were said, and done, where and when they had sex, it was right there in my hands. (Yes, he had seduced her, she fell in love with him, and then he tossed her aside. His game was complete.) When I finished reading, I didn't cry, or scream, or yell, I went cold and empty and simply handed the document back to John. He looked at me and said, "He's guilty isn't he?" and I replied, "Yes."

Anthony had been given the same document in jail earlier that day. Apparently, he knew he was caught. While still at my parent's house, the phone kept ringing, and ringing. We knew who it was, but John wanted me to read the document before talking to Anthony. After I finished reading, the phone started ringing again … it was Anthony, only this time, he had read the evidence.

When I answered, he attempted to start the same rhetoric of his innocence, but I told him that I had read the deposition. After an exhausting conversation, he finally admitted that he had been having sex with Christie for over a year … but (of course) it wasn't his fault … I was sick to my stomach! How could he do this to our best friends, who are at our home every Sunday for dinner, celebrating Christmas and birthdays? How could he look them in the eye, and hug and kiss them every time … knowing that he was having sex with their child? How could he bring her to our home and have sex in my bed while I was working at the magazine? How could he??? This man was not the man I married, not the man I knew. How could I have not spotted any of this? Why didn't anyone else? Our family was so close, we were together all the time, and no one saw this??? How is this possible?

His excuses (stories) over time went from, "she seduced me" to "it was medication I was taking"… "Mid-life crisis"…. "I was confused" … "you don't have enough sex with me and forced me into her arms"… Anthony had every reason, none of which were his fault, for having sex with a 14-year-old. (He was 47.) I filed for divorce.

In court, after testimonies and hearing Anthony talk, the judge described Anthony as a "Dr. Jekyll and Mr. Hyde" and that he apparently has never learned his lessons. When the judged asked him to explain what he had done wrong, Anthony answered, "I had an affair with Christie." The judge asked again to explain what he had done wrong, Anthony searched for an answer and said, "I had sex with Christie." The judge asked again, Anthony didn't have an answer, John leaned over and whispered to him, and then Anthony said, "I had sex with a minor child." The judge then asked, "How does a 47-year-old man manage to have sex with a 14-year-old?" A long pause, and the judge said loudly, "By seducing her!" A predator seeks out what he wants and manipulates things to get what he wants. He was sentenced eight to 20 years.

## The Unveiling

So many things took place over the years, only a few were revealed here. This last "big" event was the final straw that ended our marriage. I, nor anyone I knew, even considered for a moment that Anthony would have sex with a child. He was flirtatious and affectionate with everyone; I would suspect a woman … yes, but never a child. There is no excuse for Anthony, not one! What is scary, is that in the beginning of all this, Roberta and Mel had said to Anthony, that they thought Christie may have a little crush on him. Anthony was immediately appalled, saying, "That's not nice; that's just dirty thinking! She's like my daughter. Oh, my God, that's nasty! I would never encourage her to think. Oh, no, never!"

Roberta and Mel had to explain to Anthony that teenagers

get crushes on their teachers and mentors all the time; it was normal, and that Anthony shouldn't get upset over that, that he isn't doing anything wrong, but that he just needs to be aware of it. Little did any of us know, he had been having sex with her for months at this point! But, look at the way Anthony manipulated the situation, how he was appalled and he had to be consoled and verified that he wasn't doing anything wrong. Then saying how that was a dirty way (for people) to think, was just frightening when we looked back at this situation, and many others.

Anthony apparently believed that he could do anything in this world that he wanted ... he would justify his actions, lie, con, twist and talk his way out of anything. Only this time, he couldn't. Anthony admitted everything in court, to me, and in letters he wrote. He went to prison admitting and knowing what he did. However, still believing he could talk his way out of it, Anthony told so many stories (even in our regular life) that he actually believed his own lies. Now in prison, over the years of fabricating his case in an effort to get out, he believes he is completely innocent and that it was a major conspiracy of many people (including judges) to have him imprisoned. Anthony does not take responsibility for what he has done; he has absolutely no remorse, and has placed the blame of his incarceration, and his own actions, on everyone else. He has created his own alternative reality.

After I divorced Anthony, the next two years were full of surprises, shock, anger, as countless people came forward to tell me about the Anthony they knew. The things he had done, the women he had affairs with, the lies, the cons, the real Anthony came forward. The statement the judge had made was absolutely true, a Dr. Jekyll and Mr. Hyde. Anthony had sex and many affairs with other women during our marriage; he even had a child with another woman while we were married! I was shocked, actually horrified at how good he was at fooling everyone around him, including me, how deceitful he was.

It was horrifying when I realized I was married for 25 years to a "Social Sociopath" but I didn't know it until the very end. I told Dr. Stirling, "In looking back, there were plenty of warning signs along the way, but I had no idea what to look for."

I now know that Anthony carried over half of the traits in the Social Sociopath checklist. Seduction, Anthony seduced not only all the family with his lies and manipulation but also others for money, power, and sex. He played the victim, as nothing ever was his fault, he had an excuse for everything. He had such an air of charisma and charm that you just wanted to believe everything he said. He was a pathological liar and did not take responsibility for his actions or have the slightest care, guilt or remorse for how his actions and lies hurt others. He obviously did not even care about the consequences his actions would bring to others or himself. He could have a fit of rage in one minute and the next think everything was just fine. And the disregard for our relationship was epic and so demoralizing. I know all these years later I am still recovering from this emotional, mental and verbal abuse and total disregard and respect for our marriage. Yes, I was sucked in, under his spell, living in the illusion and didn't recognize what was happening to my life until it was too late."

When I was asked to share my story with Dr. Stirling for the purpose of helping others I realized that even after 10 years since my divorce, and surviving the devastating events in my marriage, writing my story brought up painful and humiliating feelings that I would like to have just kept buried forever. I had to go back into my past, dig deep, and bring them back to life. But I believe my experiences may help someone else to see how easily we can be manipulated and controlled by someone carrying the traits of what Dr. Stirling calls the "Social Sociopath." Watch for the signs and take this to heart, this can happen to you or a loved one.

Knowing this information has helped me to finally heal.

*Warm regards, Katherine*

# About Anthony

Anthony was the classic "Social Sociopath" acting out most of the twenty traits in Hare's checklist. From the minute she met him, she said, "He was so arrogant; it was like he was wearing a false mask, seeking attention and fame. Katherine attributed this trait to the fact that Anthony was an entertainer. But it wasn't just on stage that he desired fame and attention … it was 24/7 in every aspect of life. Everything from what he watched on television, to the music he listened to, where he went for a night out, to where he had to sit at "other people's homes" for dinner! It was always about him, life centered around Anthony, and if it didn't, his mood would change, he would be resentful, and make everyone feel as though 'they' didn't appreciate him. He manipulated situations to always be about him. He was enthralled with himself, and he considered himself a 'chick magnet.' If he wasn't thinking of ways to gain attention for himself, he was thinking, talking, watching and joking about sex.

His moods would shift on the spot and he would become angry at situations that did not even happen except in his mind. Anthony became so overconfident that he would never "get caught" because he thought he was superior to everyone else. Well, that is one "Social Sociopath" who is exactly where he belongs, behind bars being made to take responsibility for his actions.

# CHAPTER 6

---

## Case Study # 3
## I'm no Angel

My name is Terra Sinclair and early in my adult life I met the most charming young man. He was so handsome, fun and charismatic. Little did I know he had absolutely no conscience whatsoever! And, so I share my story with you in hopes this will shed light on some very dark behavior.

His name was Max and we met in class my junior year at a university of Texas. We became friends although we both had serious partners at the time. He was a year behind me but oh my what a handsome fellow! Sandy blonde hair, sparkling bright blue eyes, and tall, 6'4". (I am a sucker for tall men). I swooned instantly. I wanted to know more about him; I was drawn to him like a moth to the light. Max was funny, outgoing, charming; it seemed when he spoke to me that the rest of the world evaporated. I had his total undivided attention (I thought). I felt like a queen around him. During that semester we became good friends doing a lot of things and going out together with his frat brothers and my sorority sisters. I had been seeing someone for over two years and when we parted ways, Max was right there, "being my friend." We seemed to have so much in common.

As a new semester started, I had an unexplained fire in my apartment. My parents insisted I move back home. And, so now Max and I lived three hundred miles apart. We burned up the long distance wires although; we both now had other people in our lives. Over the next summer we both ended up working in the same city. We'd meet for lunch or drinks. He'd be all sweaty (working construction in the summer sun) he was absolutely irresistible to me. He had this power that enveloped him. A power that was so alluring, heady, addicting. I just couldn't seem to get enough. It was like being in the sun with the entire world holding it's breath watching to see what would happen next. Not only did I feel I was the center of his world, I felt like I was on stage, everyone waiting to see if I would comply. As I said, we both had other people in our lives, but I must confess I even called him while my boyfriend was in the shower one day – I just had to hear his voice. Yes, I admit I cheated on my boyfriend to become lovers with Max. I am no angel. Our friendship turned into new love, Max was fine with that arrangement as he also was "cheating" by being with me. The sex was amazing, like fireworks. It was the ultimate carnal indulgence. He talked me into experimenting in ways I've never even imagined existed. Max's motto was "If it feels good do it;" there is no right or wrong just do it.

Max was engaged but, at the end of the summer his girlfriend broke off their engagement (gee, I wonder why?) and I was his first phone call. We continued to date long distance that fall semester. Almost every weekend one of us traveled to be together. After Thanksgiving he called and asked me to move back to the university I started in. I told him the only way I would move anywhere was if I was getting married. I was

23 and now very much in love with Max. He said, "I know." Meaning yes, he knew my terms for moving back included marriage. I was unsure at first as marriage meant "forever" to me and wanted to be sure he was absolutely certain he wanted to be with me forever. I didn't believe in divorce. He assured me it would be forever. He was so convincing, almost pleading. I now know that acting so pitiful is a tactic so you feel sorry for them. It doesn't matter to them; they know they are above all others. It's just about getting what they want and at this moment, Max wanted me. Max said exactly what I needed to hear, exactly the way I needed to hear it. He always had a knack for knowing exactly what to say to hook me completely. It's a gift, I guess, and Max had it. He was a master of manipulation.

So, I packed up and moved even though I was in the middle of my senior year. Back to my sorority and a very familiar world. Max and I became the couple on campus, no small accomplishment on a campus with nearly 20,000 students. Strangers would say 'hi' to us as we were walking to class and comment on what a perfect couple we made. Everyone said we even looked alike; we could pass for brother and sister. We got an apartment together. His parents hit the fan. They said," absolutely not, their son would not live in sin, what would other people think? So we paid for a second apartment. Perfectly empty but we had two addresses, whoopee. Considering we were struggling students, the expense was silly… and unfair; my dad paid for gasoline for both of us. Max was very willing to accept the help.

That spring, we were engaged. The day of our engagement we had our first real fight. I wasn't certain I locked my car door and he made me go check. We never worried about locks and I couldn't understand why Max was being so nasty about it. Little did I know the ring was in the car. He showed me how horrid he could be, the real him for just a brief moment. My feelings were hurt but I still said "yes." After all, I believed this man to be the catch. He was handsome, smart, charming, witty, and powerful. I felt beautiful and wanted with him, I felt like he had eyes for no one but me. That he'd be a perfect father and excellent provider as everything he touched turned to gold. In the weeks and months that followed I began to feel another reality unfolding, I had become a trophy, on display wherever we went. And, when he looked at me with that intense smile, I could feel some dark perverse thoughts going through his head and it was quite chilling for me. Yet, I said nothing. I could also see he gave other women the same look.

When we announced our engagement to his family, his mother called me a whore in front of his entire family. He said nothing, did nothing. I was so stunned that I just sat there. I cried silently over my salad. Already his undermining of my confidence was at work. Any normal person would have left immediately.

Due to moving back and forth between universities, I ended up going an extra semester. As he was a year behind me, that worked out well for both of us. I went to work full time in Retail. Even though I worked 50 hours a week, I loved it!

Since I worked most Saturdays that played perfectly into Max's secret life. He had plenty of free time without me around. Soon other co-eds were calling him frequently.

There was one in particular; Max was so arrogant he told me about it. (Testing to see how I'd react. I believed males and females could be "just friends" so I naively thought nothing about it.) I suggested he invite her and her beau to join us for dinner sometime (little did I know Max was the beau!). She finally stopped calling after another month or so.

Then his professor lent him her car. Now, why on earth would a professor lend their car to a student? There was nothing wrong with his car but she "traded" with him for awhile. His story was so convincing – quite convoluted about how he had helped the professor with placing other students into internships and how it was important that he present a certain image as a sales person, that her car presented a better image of success. I knew how important image was to Max so I bought the story as truth.

Even though I had graduated, I was still doing assignments ... his assignments. "Because you're so much better at writing than I am," he'd say. I earned an "A" in Marketing 402 and I wasn't even enrolled in university any longer much less a business major.

Max was great at getting others to do things for him. He was an expert at the art of persuasion. Max would use whatever was necessary to convince you of whatever it is he wanted. It was like a game for Max, "Let's see if I can get her to do X." At first, they start off small and slow. Then Max would get me to do something he knows was against my values. He tested to find my weak spot and then once found, he exploited it. I know I allowed this to happen but by now I was not even the vibrant girl I was just a year back. I was a very attractive young woman and I knew it. Max played that against me, always making certain I never felt "good enough" or "perfect enough" to be with him. So, little by little, I became less sure of myself and thought it was me who was "less than." After years of listening to bits of criticism, my self-confidence withered away to nothing.

"This is the classic combination of Verbal, emotional and mental abuse that is present with the social sociopathic behavior."

Our wedding was approaching fast and I wanted a very pale pink wedding dress. I don't look good in white and to be honest, I did not feel it appropriate. But again, he talked me into a white dress saying he loved me in white. I suggested a cream, and he insisted on white. When his mother discovered I would be wearing a white dress, she said, "Well, if she can wear white, so can I," and she did. In a brief moment of sanity, I understood that was a reflection on her, not me. Blessedly, no one ever said a word about it to me. But, he insisted I wear white because he knew it would set off his mother. Max both hated his mother deeply and yet loved her. He did little things to get even with her and yet he always sought her approval, which he never received.

He grew up with that sort of mother. She never ever forgot a word you said. Three years later she'd bring up the tiniest off-handed remark you made. I never had to watch what I said to anyone before. What an eye opener! She was not a nice person – she was very unhappy with life. She took it out on everyone around her including Max whenever she had the opportunity.

Control seemed to be the new mantra for Max. The entire world was his puppet theatre and the game is to see who he can get to do what. He was a master of manipulation, master of persuasion, and a natural born liar if there is such a thing. Max was very, very smart but to him a lie meant nothing. Knowing what I know now, I do not know how he remembered all the lies and all the stories and kept them straight.

When we had been married for three years, I found out that my darling husband had a daughter, a 2-year-old daughter! Do the math; notice it doesn't quite work does it? Barely three months into our marriage, he was having affairs and got another woman pregnant. Remembering back, Max said he wanted to get away for a few days and was going to Mexico with some buddies. Well, I found some photos of Max in Mexico with his "buddies"... problem was, there were no "buddies" only a very pregnant woman by his side. Yes, this was one of his girlfriends and she was pregnant.

When I first found out about his daughter, I believed that two people who loved each other could overcome anything. I went into therapy. My therapist asked, "Do you feel like you have done everything to make the marriage work?" I answered "No." I called his best friend. I told him he must know that things were not going well with our marriage and would he please tell me anything that would help.

He said, "Well, you know he's a serious business man, so write things out where he can understand them, make a business plan for your marriage." So, I wrote a 30-page business plan. I presented it to him when he returned from a work trip. He flipped through the pages, set it on the desk and never looked at it again. Now I could say "yes," I have tried everything.

We had been married for about four years and a co-worker of Max's hurt her back while in training at corporate headquarters. I insisted she move into our home and I cared for her until her back healed, especially since she was nearly a thousand miles from home. She was there four weeks. It was afterwards that I learned she had also been one of his lovers. After staying at our house, she realized what was really going on and how Max was lying to every one, she told me that Max had seduced her and others at the office and that he had many others in his "secret life." She turned on him and became vigilant at warning other women within the corporation to what sort of person he really was. She was one of my greatest cheerleaders. I thank her for helping me to wake up to the hell I was living.

Max's job required him to travel five days a week for over half the year. How handy for him! After our divorce, the ex-girlfriends starting coming out of the woodwork! They were my best allies as they had been jilted and screwed royally by him. His ex-harem included one of my closest friends, one of the bridesmaids at our wedding. She was vulnerable and apparently the handiest person to conquer. It took me years to forgive her but then I realized she was as much a victim as I.

On my 28th birthday Max took me to dinner, gave me a beautiful gold watch and then asked for a divorce – four days shy of our fifth anniversary. (He had to ask on my birthday?

He couldn't have picked any other day? Typical, the only people they think of is themselves … ever.) The upcoming anniversary was particularly significant because we had made a pact to wait five years before having children. We wanted to have nice things and a comfortable home before having children. We had achieved all that and he knew I always wanted children. The photo of his 4-year-old daughter came in real handy during our divorce. I moved home to pick up the pieces but retained right of first refusal on the house.

In all our time together he never laid a hand on me. One time he did throw the phone at me hitting the doorframe. I told him the next time I would call the police. He never did it again. Sometimes the worst abuse is the kind that leaves no visible wounds, no physical bruises. How can you explain to anyone the terror you live with daily, the pain and the constant criticism? The snide comments, being purposely embarrassed in public, constantly humiliated, manipulated? Until we met, I had always been a strong personality. And ready with an opinion for just about anything. The day I woke up, the day I knew this was really over, was the day someone asked me what I thought about something and I said, "Gee, I don't really have any opinion about that." I had some how lost myself, confused and devastated I still stayed with him.

When I found myself behaving like his mother, cataloging and storing up things he said as future ammunition, even then I stayed. I was beyond miserable. And at that point, I believed this was how life was, how it was suppose to be. He had me convinced that I lived to make him happy and when I failed, I was a failure, useless and damn lucky he kept me around. That's the most amazing aspect of this to me, how do they get you to want to do things for them?

Dr. Stirling shared with me " The only law is their law; the only rules are their rules; and it is all just a game. Once they tire of the toy, it is tossed aside without a second thought. Once conquered, it's on to new challenges."

I grieved and pined for Max for 10 years after we divorced. He was my true love I thought. I had given him everything I could and he left me an empty shell. It was another 10 years (20 total) before I really began to heal the wounds inflicted on me. I was a naïve, loving, hopeful young woman and I turned into a distrustful, codependent shell of a human at his skilled hand. I completely understand that I allowed it to happen, that I was a willing victim. But it was not conscious. I never even imagined this sort of person ever existed much less that I would run into one. I now see how sociopaths suck you in and tangle you in their web of lies and games until you cannot tell up from down, right from wrong, dark from light. And when they're done with the game, you're just road kill tossed aside.

After our divorce Max called me and wanted to meet with me – he wouldn't tell me why. Curiosity got the best of me and I went. He wanted me to sign the title on the house because he had sold it. There on the deed was his name and the name of my best friend from college, as his wife. I asked, "Is that the Debbie I know?" He said, "Yes." And I told him, "You know, I could easily refuse to sign this document and instead have you thrown in jail for breaking the divorce decree. You are required by law to notify me of your intent to sell and give me first option to buy. You have no idea of my situation and you have denied me that right." Inside I was shaking so bad I was almost faint but, watching him turn ghost white at the thought of jail (ah, I finally found what he was afraid of!) made it all worth it. After six and half years together, I finally won one against him! Wooo hooo!

Max could always sell anything to anybody; he had no conscience, no scruples. I've always said he could sell deep freezers to Eskimos; no offense intended, it's just he was that good at twisting people into doing what ever it was he wanted. And he made you want to do it!

In five years of marriage we moved five times cross-country. I know of at least twenty women who were his lovers, some for a short time and some a bit longer but none more than a year. The mother of his daughter really thought he'd marry her when we divorced but of course he didn't.

The signs were there although; he did a really good job of covering his tracks. I only found out for certain when he got careless. And I believe he wanted me to know. It was another test. Would I stick around? None of the women were enough of a challenge until we moved back to the part of the country where we went to university. He hooked up with our old lab partner and one of my best friends. Unbeknownst to me, they decided to both get divorced so they could get married. Apparently she believed him over me all those years. I don't blame her; I myself was in her shoes. I believe he is on wife four or five now.

In hindsight there were many subtle warnings over the years.

There were many opportunities to escape. I almost didn't go through with the wedding. Denial is not just a river in Egypt. And through denial we can refuse to see, to hear, and even feel what is real. We can create a make-believe world to safely hide within. But eventually, the walls of glass shatter and when they do it is particularly painful.

Today, I am in a very healthy relationship. With a man I trust emphatically. A man who treats me as his equal. And whom I know loves me no matter what. I am a wiser woman now.

Women, please be careful out there, the recovery is long and hard after an encounter with one of these Conscienceless creatures.

*All my best, Terra*

# About Max

Max was a real charmer and such a great liar. He was so good at keeping everything separate. Terra said, "It is hard to believe he even had a child with another woman while we were married. I bet she knew nothing of me just like I was supposed to know nothing about her. The pain and anguish in a relationship where everything is a calculated lie is devastating."

Max, as it turned out, never even stopped dating the girls from college even after he was married to Terra and living the "good" life. The life he said he wanted. Terra said, "When he showed up at my door after our divorce with his new wife, one of my friends from college, you could have blown me over with a feather. I knew instantly that this affair was probably going on the whole time we were married." Terra had the opportunity to read this book before publication. She said to you readers, "Please take heed to what has been written in this book. It can happen to you as easily as it happened to me."

"Sometimes you can be in the right place at the right time and be so preoccupied with old habits and patterns that you miss the opportunity that was meant for you."

**SZS**

# CHAPTER 7

---

# Case Study #4
# Terrible Ted

I shared with Dr. Stirling that I was 24 years old when I met Ted. He was charming and handsome and very generous. Ted acted like a man in love. He would look at me with such affection in his eyes it would just melt me. We dated for about three and a half years. He treated me like I hung the moon, meaning the sun rose and set by my command. I was impressed with Ted and he showered me with gifts and that really made me feel special. He came from a family with money and he seemed to have plenty as well. He had a video production company and it was successful. Maybe I fell in love for the wrong reasons, but it felt so right at the time. I thought he would be a good provider and that was important to me. We had what I thought was a good relationship. However, that good relationship started changing just months after we moved in together. Small things at first. For example, one time, only months into our relationship, Ted grew angry with me for taking too much room on the couch. He started "playing" push-me-push-you with his feet. Soon, he kicked so hard that I was pushed off the couch onto the floor. He played it off, as did his mother who had watched, but it felt like a violent act to me. I just brushed it off as no one else seemed to be making a fuss over it. This was the only clue in three and a half years of dating and I blew it off as a one-time act. We were married on a cool fall day on Maui. I was at that time literally barefoot (on the beach) and pregnant (seven months). All went well... for a while.

Our first son was born about three months after we married. Up until then Ted seemed to be able to control his outbursts, it was about a week after our first son was born when Ted began openly displaying his dark side. He refused to help with the baby and any duties associated with the child. But when his family and friends were around, he would do anything and everything for the boy. Even change diapers. He was the epitome of the good daddy. The helpful hubby. The loving man. When people left our home, it was back to Ted the Terror who didn't help and who was now being verbally abusive.

The verbal abuse suddenly turned to physical violence one day when Ted felt I wasn't helping him find his wallet. Here is what happened … Ted was having what I would call one of his dark moments. He walked into the living room and announced that he needed help finding his wallet. I didn't say a word, but instead got up from the couch where I was holding the baby and put the baby in his playpen. I then started walking down the hall. Ted perceived this as an act of defiance or aggression and rushed up behind me, yelling that I was a horrible person (not his real words – they were much worse) for not helping and how could I just walk out of the room. I was about to turn around and tell him to calm down because I was going to the bedroom to look. Ted kicked me so hard in the leg that it left a bruise from the top of my knee to just under my rear end. I fell to the floor; it hurt bad.

I started to cry while Ted yelled at me to get up and that I'm not hurt. I was hurt, but not just my leg. That day I realized I was living with a crazy man, someone who could ACT like a normal, loving man to the outside world and who was actually a violent, abusive man at home behind closed doors. I decided then to get out of the marriage, but that proved much more difficult than I could have imagined.

Eventually I moved out and was living in an apartment with my first son. I was filing for divorce. Ted came to my apartment wanting to discuss our relationship, telling me he didn't want a divorce and that he could change. He was calm and charming, so I let him in. He continued to turn on the charm. We opened a bottle of wine. I let his charm take me over and as a result our second child was conceived. Ted could be the most charming man alive when he wanted to be. He later told me that the evening was planned out, that he decided to create that second child, that he had decided nothing would stop him from giving our first boy a sibling. I believe, looking back, that if I had said no, Ted would have become aggressive. Ted knew the second child would drive me back into the marriage and he was right. I felt obligated. I had no support and was struggling financially. Ted was doing extremely well financially. I hate that I went back, but I did. I am not a victim. I made my choices.

Ted viewed me as his possession and he did not seem to

understand boundaries. He was above all the mundane rules. Months after we had separated for our fourth and final time, Ted rented an apartment far from my home. It was a relief. However, he would show up unannounced and walk into my home. Living in the mid west we never lock our doors. Ted would show up uninvited and want to start a fight. I was resolved to not participate in his crazy-making behavior at any cost; he would usually give up and leave.

Ted's behavior lasted through the years off and on. One instance sticks in my mind, and this came after our final separation – 20 years into our knowing each other. About three months after Ted left our home after I had filed for the divorce he continued the pop-by visits. We didn't always have the doors locked so he took full advantage. On this occasion, I was in the shower. I didn't know he was in the house. My older boys were really upset, but I remained calm as Ted unlocked the bathroom door and stepped into the shower with me. I was shocked but knew I had to remain calm. I had learned to fear his anger and split-second mood changes, and knew remaining calm was important. He wouldn't act out so strongly if I remained calm. I talked him out of the shower. It was unbelievable to me that he thought this behavior was okay. I put on a robe and offered calmly and quietly to call the police. He left. It was a very odd incident to share with you here, but it makes a point about boundaries. He just seems to think I am a possession. I feel like I have to keep my doors locked, though he no longer just drops by. Ted has a live-in girlfriend who keeps him occupied. I am no longer the main object of his "affections."

Ted was very smart. He seemed to know my moves before even

I did. He perceived my leaving (before our final separation I left him three times) as acts of undeniable disloyalty. It felt like he was on guard around me. After the earlier incident I shared with you, when he kicked me for not helping him find his wallet, I was able to leave the following afternoon when he was out. I packed quickly, grabbed by child and headed to my family who lived in another city. I didn't make it. I got as far as the next town before Ted the Charmer and his mother talked me into coming back "home." Things were right as rain for maybe a year after that. Then his strange behaviors started again. I left again, this time locally. That's when I took an apartment in the same city. Ted promised to seek help and we did go to counseling, treating the issues as a couple, but it was not a couples issue; it was Ted. Ted was clearly out of control with anger and lashing out. Soon after is when other episodes occurred and I moved to an apartment with my boy.

As you recall from my earlier description, during this separation, Ted was good and turned back to his charming self. He used that charm to get into my apartment and into my head. He made me believe that he was making strides and changing. He also used his charm to create our second son. I moved back into our home when I learned I was pregnant. Again, things went well for some time. I separated from Ted again when my second child was about 18 months old. I moved out this time with my two boys.

I found a cute little cottage where I lived with my sons not far from their father. While we were separated Ted brought gifts, food, all of our furniture to my new little cottage. He kept telling me about his counseling, his treatment, and his life. I didn't believe any of it. I didn't let him in … until about a year into the separation and after he had gone away to work on himself in Hawaii.

As Ted showed signs of major improvement, we began to talk again and spend a little time together. We again sought therapy together. The therapist suggested that we could try the family again but that we would have to move away from the area (we lived in L.A. at the time) and start over completely. We would have to pretend to love each other. Fake it till it's real. Horrible advice, looking back. It worked for seven years, however, with no acts of violence. Ted's secret life continued. I didn't learn that until our divorce years later. The things I've learned since don't shock me. They don't phase me. That he was secretly seeking out couples to have sex with, that he watched gay porn, that he hung out at strip clubs, that he had a secret library of the world's nastiest porn and that he lied consistently about where he was and what he was doing came as no surprise. I found out he was using a variety of drugs including meth and cocaine. I warned him that his actions were not conducive to a marriage and family life. He thought I would back down as I normally did, but now that my children (now three of them) were getting older, I could no longer put them through this dysfunctional existence. I wasn't playing the game any longer. Ted had to go.

We stayed married for sixteen years, give or take a few, and as I look back I know I stayed about ten yeas too many. I found out about that time he had a fling with my best friend and with a frequent female visitor to his home after we separated the second time. It was rumored that he was "dating" an 18-year-old girl in the neighborhood, too. I simply didn't care at that point. Ted had no conscience and had to always be right. It was like he was the only one he felt needed respect and consideration. Our relationship was a hideous roller coaster and I am just grateful beyond words to have gotten off that toxic ride.

Ted had no conscious about his actions, about all the harm he caused. He continues not to take responsibility for his actions and to tell me that I am the bad one who victimized him. He tells me to this day that he didn't do the things I caught him doing and that he was not as bad as I make him out to be. And he tells me that anything he may have done, these acts of violence, his outbursts and his lies, cheating … that everything is MY fault. He smiles when he says this.

Who has changed is ME and my beliefs. I do not believe him or anything he says. His children do not believe him. He lost the love of his older boys and currently is doing anything and everything in his power to make our youngest boy, now 12, think that he hangs the moon. He bestows many gifts at my son's feet. He takes him out to dinner a lot. He tells him he loves him, which he just might for real. But he still lies. He still forgets to do things he promises the boy. He still disappears. He is not abusive, which is interesting. He knows that upon the very first instance of verbal abuse I will yank custody so fast that it will make his head spin and that I will call Social Services. Ted has a lot to lose. He blames me for the loss of his older sons' love and respect. Ted doesn't see that they witnessed his actions, and they saw the damage. They saw the bruises and cuts after Ted was through venting his rage on me. I am a down-to-earth, independent woman who would have told you in a heartbeat that this could never happen to me, but it did, so please be careful out there and know that this behavior and abuse does not get better, only worse as time goes on. I am grateful to be able to share my story and if it helps even one person to live a happier, smarter life, that would mean the world to me.

*That's all for now, Sarah*

# About Ted

Ted crosses the line into the "Purest Sociopath" by acting out his rage on others he erases the boundary that keeps the "Social Sociopath" from being physically abusive. This is a key component to the difference between the purest and the social sociopath. Ted was the classic bully, spoiled and used to having his own way. His parents covered up his abusive behavior and he never learned that his actions would bring consequences. Ted is a dangerous man because he was never told or shown that his behavior was unacceptable to society. He does his best to hide his brutality but he is not in control on so many levels. Sarah was lucky to get out of this alive. Sarah shared with me that Ted's whole family had no idea what boundaries meant.

There is little hope that Ted will ever be fit for a relationship and I am fairly certain if we keep an eye on his future he will one day make the news and not in a good way. The very first time you feel fear of abuse in any form, the very first time some one has such total disregard for you that they think it is ok to hit you or kick you that needs to be the last time you allow yourself to be alone with your abuser ever! And, yes, report any abuse to the police; it is just the smart thing to do.

Sarah shared with me that one final and very severe act of

violence came at the hands of Ted … eight months after their final separation had begun. Ted brutally beat Sarah while keeping her captive in his apartment. When Sahara escaped she went to the police immediately and Ted was arrested for false imprisonment and assault, but these charges were dropped down to misdemeanor and domestic violence as unbelievable as that sounds. Ted was on medication for ADD and had been drinking. Ted was extremely good at hiding the truth, he didn't appear to be drunk or affected. In fact, he seemed fine, said Sarah. She admits that putting herself alone with this person wasn't the best move, but she didn't expect the outcome. "He was on me, punching me and throwing me around the apartment, in about two minutes. I didn't see it coming."

# CHAPTER 8

---

# Conversations, Tidbits & Moments of Truth While in Relation with Steven, Anthony, Max & Ted

It is rare indeed that one can sit and have a conversation with a social sociopath about his sociopathic behavior. I was no threat, intrigued and sincere and calm, Steven knew I was not inclined to reaction so when I asked very nicely if we could have a conversation, that there were a few things I needed cleared up and would he help me, he said yes. (At this moment I became an audience for his drama, an extension to the game. It was all about him and he loved the attention and so he shared some truths with me.) We sat on the couch and I asked, "Can we have a few moments of truth?" Steven agreed and with no emotion I said, "It seems there are so many wild stories that we both know are not true, and lately you have not even looked me in the eye so would it be ok if we removed some of the wedges these lies have caused?"

Steven said okay.

I said, "Thank you. I appreciate this."

So, I asked about one of the times he disappeared for two days while up in Canada working. I was so worried of course and then he called and he told me he was on a boat with 14 guys, the story was so ridiculous I asked, "What was that about?"

Steven laughed and said, "That was a lie. I was in Vancouver with Elaine; we had a blast and I was so drunk by the time I spoke to you I was back in Surrey at Home Depot." I still had no expression except a smile and said, "Oh. Thank you. That makes so much more sense."

Then I asked, "What about the time you disappeared and surfaced a day later and told me you were arrested for not having your passport on you?"

Again he laughed, "Yeah, that was a lie as well. I was with Chressa."

I asked if he had others in our bed up in Canada.

He said, "Yes, a number of times." Still no emotion from me as I thanked him.

I knew from the phone bill he had called some prostitutes off of Craigslist.

"Yes, I called and had a conversation with one of them."

I asked like a questioning child, "Did you really have prostitutes over to the house?"

He said, "Yes, but not for me; I had a friend over." I just

smiled and knew it was a lie but at least he was truthful about the call.

He looked me in the eye. I said, "See! Doesn't that feel better? He shrugged his shoulders and said, "I need another Vodka." We went on with our evening as if we had just talked about the weather.

We went to a birthday party, it was a beautiful summer night and all our friends were there. During the party we talked to many people, after a conversation Steven would say, "Yeah, I had sex with her!" or someone would come up and hug him and he would look at me and smile, I would smile back. Steven got very drunk that evening, having maybe a dozen vodkas.

On the way home he said, "I cannot believe that I have had sex with at least six women at that party." I calmly looked at him and said; "Yes, Honey, you are a slut, and what's more you are a pathological liar." He just looked at me, but said no more. We hit a drive-thru so he could get a hamburger but by the time we got close to home I had to pull over in a parking lot so he could vomit. I mean really, it was like Junior High. Is any of this sounding familiar?

Once in a while Steven would look at me and say, "You handle me pretty well." I would just smile and inside I would be thinking, "This is so sick, and I am living in this illusion – am I sick too?" I just said, "This is too small for me and your 19-year-old behavior is not so cute for a man of 55 years. But it is not my job to judge you." And I meant that with all my heart.

# Tidbits

*(Fist hand clues from Steven, Anthony, Max and Ted)*

It is rare that one gets to have moments of truth when in conversation with a person who looks at life as a game and lies even when there is no need.

"If you are there at the right time and right place and you listen, amazing and compelling truths may be found.

One evening Steven and I were in the kitchen he looked at me with loving eyes and said, "Sheri, I love you so much," and I said, "And sometimes you hate me for it." His eyes still had the look of love but were ice cold as he said, "YES! Sometimes I hate you for it." (I now know that was the truth, the frightening and chilling truth.)

What does it take to brag about going to a friend's birthday party and while he is upstairs blowing out candles you're downstairs banging his wife on his desk. (It takes no conscience and craving the high of "getting away with it" it takes having no thought or care of the consequence to either person, it takes a bit of Sociopathic behavior, yes?)

One morning we were getting dressed and Steven looked at me and said, "I am the best liar in the world." I looked up, smiled and said, "Yes, Dear, I know."

While out to dinner at the Four Seasons, sitting at the bar, Steven looked me right in the eye and said seriously, "Sheri, please know I do love you. Please listen to my words and not my actions." I was taken back and knew he was warning me in some way, I would like to think he was trying to protect me but I know that is my illusion.

I said, "Honey, that is just bullshit, your actions will always speak louder than your words."

When sharing and talking about his escapades Steven would proudly say, "They are the last to know." I smiled as I had already been getting the phone bills. It was the only way for me to know the truth and not be "the last to know."

One week Steven came to me and said, "I'm trying to change you too much." The next week he came and said, "I am trying to change too much, I am not this domesticated." I thought, "Domesticated? With 13 girls in rotation? I think not!" I knew he was looking for a way out but I was not going to make it easy. He would have to make the move.

There was a girl in Canada he used to call all the time. Her name is Elaine. Then there were no calls for about eight months, then the phone number showed up on his phone a few times and I called it. It was the same girl who answered and it was now a catering business that happened to be the same catering business that the owners of the house in Canada use for their bigger parties. It seems to me that Steven put her in business and since he makes all the catering plans … Hey, what could be more cozy? What do you think? Did he put her in business or is it just a coincidence?

On one of Steven's trips, he picked up a woman in the airport on the way back to Canada. He kept telling me how wonderful she and her husband were and how much he liked them and wanted us all to get together and have dinner the next time I came to visit him in Canada. He said they owned a restaurant in Vancouver and told me the name of it; he said he had great times there. I noticed he started spending more nights up in Vancouver. I did a bit of research and found out that there was this great restaurant in Vancouver, but what a surprise it was owned by a single woman who was often referenced as "the wild one." Just one more deception or so he thought.

I used to say, "Hey! He has all the vodka he can drink, all the money he can spend and all the women he can hunt. Why should he want to change a thing? At least thirteen women in rotation and one or two favorites to focus on, know even if he marries the behavior does NOT change."

I did not know Steven had told his boss "we were taking a break." He got very upset, outraged really that I would be in contact with "his" people. I brought them a Christmas card and some cookies, and just left them on their doorstep. I had no idea they knew. And I had no idea what had been said, as they would not even acknowledge the gift. It was Christmas after all and they had been so kind and gracious to me over the years. I was now alone and had lots of time to make cookies and cards and do my best to be in the holiday spirit. The spirit of grateful giving.

Anthony was self absorbed, and was often boasting about sexual behaviors. He was practically addicted to the porn channels, and once he had discovered how to use a computer, he would be surfing for hours. Is your honey working or surfing? That is the question!

Over the years it is difficult for even very smart people to keep track of all their lies. Eventually you'll notice that things aren't "jiving." Follow your instincts … you're right and they're lying! That is what happened with Max, he got more and more carless.

"At first Max only had eyes and ears for me," shared Terra. "When we were dating it felt like I had his undivided attention. Once we were married all pretense dropped, I was now officially his possession. Before we were married he'd tell me how nice I looked when we were about to go out. After marriage he'd find anything to criticize. 'Why didn't you polish your nails?' or 'You haven't shaved today' or 'Your hair looks dead.' Anything to make certain I knew I was damn lucky to be with him despite my severe shortcomings. (After a while, even I began to feel it was true)."

If singles (and even married) persons of the opposite sex seem to flock to your special person and they bask in it, you could have a sociopath on your hands. Even when we were at the hardware store in work clothes, women would turn from what they're doing for a second glance at Max. He was like a huge magnet and Max always had time to flirt even when I was right by his side.

When buying things to decorate his new office, Max bought a new coffee mug. It said, "Life's a Bitch & Then You Marry One."

When Max was in town, Terra and he went to dinner with his

friends from work nearly every weekend. The couple didn't have any other friends and her friends weren't welcome. There were couples and individuals. No one would talk to Terra beyond common courtesy. They were probably afraid they'd slip and reveal Max's indiscretions.

At social functions for Max's business, most of the female co-workers and the wives of the male co-workers were always especially nice to Terra even though they had never met. She said that she always thought that was curious. After divorcing she realized they all knew Max had many other female interests and they felt sorry for her! She found out Max's co-workers knew plenty and the men shared it with their wives and the women were oh so nice to Terra. But not one person called to let her know what they knew.

Sarah says that to this day Ted tells her that he didn't do the things she caught him doing and that he was not as bad as she makes him out to be. Sarah warns all women to stand your ground, you are not crazy, and the man is just in denial of any wrongdoing.

Sarah adds, "I tried so many times to leave. Ted would charm me back. There were always good reasons to return and I see now there is no good reason for staying with someone who is abusive in any way. It is toxic to the children as well as yourself.

How crazy does some one have to be to be beating his spouse up and calmly take a phone call in the middle of it, sounding normal and sweet and then hang up the phone and continue beating the one person in his life he claimed to love.

It is amazing how fast time flies and one day you look back on your life and realize how devastating staying in a relation with someone who carries these traits can be. You may break free but the recovery is a long road back. I would have liked to have known what I know now and been able to stop the train wreak before it got started."

*"It's not about the event...*

*it's about our perception of the event and*

*how we react to it"*

**SZS**

# CHAPTER 9

---

# Did I attract this?

We have all been taught that we attract all that comes into our world. That when we are ready to learn a teacher will appear. I tend to look at things a bit differently. Do I believe the law of attraction? Yes! However, did you attract this or were you being hunted? Pursued by a masterful predator and so went willingly down the path of love and illusion. I do believe in catalysts. That when we are ready willing and able to either let go of a false belief or block about ourselves that a catalyst will appear in our life and help the transformation. Were we looking for love? Were we enjoying the attention? Were we so willing to slip into the silky illusion? For most of us the answer would be yes, willing victims, as they say.

But I do not believe in being a victim. I believe in seeking and living in truth, allowing myself to grow and expand from every life experience. How about you? Are you wiser now? Are you finding new and healthy ways to work through the pain, hurt and disappointment when one of these creatures' leave? When a catalyst comes along, maybe it is time to look within, to once again blossom into what is to be. It is said, "The best revenge is to live well." Go beyond the circumstance and embrace your growth, your new and wonderful life, your freedom from the illusion. Know you did not cause this mess. You were part of the story; it was exciting while the love was fresh and new. Were their positive changes in your life? Look for the blessing in every event and you will surely receive the gift of serenity and hope for a brighter and more meaningful future.

# CHAPTER 10

---

# Secret Life of a
# Social Sociopath

Oh, yes, there is a secret life ... one that does not include you. As long as he or she is able to keep up their secret life, with no interference, the sociopath will appear fairly normal. It is likely that these other women or men do not even know you exist. The secret proves to the sociopath again and again how superior he or she is and how they are above any rules or agreements as it pertains to a relationship. It helps them to carry out the illusion that they are super beings, and the rest of us are fools to be played. I want to think that so much of this is unconscious to them that they are just doing what they have always done.

Like a ride at the carnival these sociopaths just do not know how to get off. But the truth is that is my illusion and they as everybody else have the opportunity to change for the better in their lives. The secret life is all-important to someone caring the traits of a Social Sociopath. It is an integral piece in their seemingly complicated puzzle. I say seemingly because it enhances the thrill to be complicated for the Social Sociopath. To look so simple on the outside, but inside nothing could be further from the truth. In truth it is simple. These social predators are often driven by their infancy needs, they have dug a hole so deep in denial that everything is calculatingly justified in their minds, they see and like to be "the good guy" not realizing that they become their on cliché. Their skill has become masterful and they breeze through their life unconsciously or consciously wreaking havoc and destruction for all who get close. It's a dichotomy really. They hunt what they feel they must have, love, affection, loyalty, and commitment. When this has been accomplished they move to the next phase. To control, diminish, and destroy that which they put their whole life effort into attaining. Their constant flow of new games keeps them from feeling and when they begin to really feel they throw the switch, walk away, and go on to the new and shinny game as they cannot stand and will not look at or take responsibility for the mess they leave. They want the best of everything and when things get a bit rocky they flee. They believe they are the hero, but underneath they know they are the villain, and so the play goes on and on, their strength is in their secret, keeping all the many games secret from each other and so insuring they will always have a back up for their back up. They live in the delusion that this actually works for them, having the best of each conquest and then tossing out the remains of their carnage. They believe their secret life is working for them, so why change?

# CHAPTER 11

# A Betrayal of Innocence

What makes encounters or relationships with a social sociopath so devastating?

I believe love is the purest form of innocence. When we are in love we are in the "divine trance." Our heart is open and we have allowed ourselves to become vulnerable, like a child, believing in our heart and soul that this beautiful human out of all the other humans has opened there heart and soul to us, allowed themselves to be vulnerable to us. We have used all of our senses and our body, mind and spirit has approved this one being, this one person to come in. We invited them in and here we are like an innocent child, arms and heart open wide.

We inherently think that all beings are "like us" with a heart and a soul and a mind and a conscience. All humans are alike in this way, or so we thought and so we were taught.

Like a young child who has been abused by a parent or family member, the wounds go deep because our family is like the core of our world. They are on the inside of us in all we say, feel and do. These precious few people that will journey with us through life help to mold who and how we are as beings on this planet. We learn right and wrong from them and learn our first boundaries from our family. When moral, spiritual, mental, or physical boundaries are broken by our family it is nothing less than a betrayal of the child's innocence and all that the purest form of love has and is.

It is as adults, when we are in love, that we become closer to the divine child within, which affects all we say, think, and do.

When the "relationship" has ended with one of these stunning predators we ask why this hurt is so intense? Why is this so bewildering and unraveling? Why am I so dismantled and devastated?

The answer to that question lay within the methods used in the hunting and capturing process. We were quietly and unknowingly being manipulated into placing this being as "family" beneath and deeper than most relationships. All the truths that we have believed in become lies. We opened our hearts and the deep places reserved for "family." The places that touch the deepest part of our humanness … our being-ness. It is nothing less than the betrayal of innocence and at its core lies a broken heart and dismantling bewilderment.

Think about it! Why does it feel so much more than hurt feelings? Was it our own expectation that betrayed us? These are some of the reflective questions that may arise after being "close" with a social sociopath. This is what makes them so dangerous to anyone who is taken in and eventually offered up as a sacrifice to their hidden agenda. It is not our expectations unless you include taking for granted that all people are human. Humans have a conscience, a sense of right and wrong, a sense of caring, a sense of others and an understanding that each heart is fragile and precious. It knows about the unseen sign or poster (if you will) that lies over each heart that says "Handle with care."

We have learned to protect our heart in so many ways, some healthy and some maybe not so healthy. Bare in mind and take it to heart that you were being human. You may have chosen poorly like a young child or new lamb, your heart was full of love and you became the innocent once again. You immersed yourself in what was shown and told to you as truth, only to realize that each truth was really a lie. (LIE = Love Is Ended)

You cannot truly love and respect someone, look into that person's eyes and lie. Having respect and caring for another's heart is all part of what goes on beneath the surface of relationship. It is at the core of every human relationship.

When our innocence is betrayed it is devastating. Not only has love ended, but also we realize that for the most part, all we were living while in this love was a lie. Whether for a week, a month, a year or many years, coming out of a "relationship" with a Social Sociopath is not easy and will require you to really learn to love yourself again, to not take the blame or responsibility that your so called "loved one" did not take. Yes, it's a train wreck and will take some time to clear away.

For it is more than your heart that has been betrayed. It is your innocence itself that took the blow. So take your time; heal your precious heart.

I used to ask myself, "If this means so little to him, why

does it mean so much to me?" The answer is that like you I am human. I have a heart that opened to the innocence of love and that innocence, that open heart was broken, the innocence betrayed, the caring for all others was interrupted and questioned. So, now we will be more cautious, keep our radar on, seek the true humans. KNOW THIS: You are a miraculous being, capable of healing your heart, regaining your innocence and loving once again.

# CHAPTER 12

# Red Flags & Insights for Your Continued Well-Being

*Red Flags come in varying degrees*

With raging and physical abuse, it may not take long for the abusive person to tip their hand. But with verbal, mental, and emotional abuse, especially subtle forms: criticism through implication, withholding, abusive "jokes," unilateral decisions, innuendos coated with charm, and a "what-are-you-complaining-about" attitude, you may not know a red flag was waved. In addition the "Social Sociopath" knows how to control the rage and all that is shown to you is the sweet caring person, that is until you get "in relation" with them.

With some abusers depending on the individual, they may tip their hand early on. They will say or do something that will cause a red flag to go up and we would hope at that point you would say thank you but no thank you. The same goes for controlling behavior. Someone who is controlling will sometimes quickly begin to want to control you and again this may be the point you will choose to say thank you but, no thank you. It is quite different with the social predator. He is a skilled hunter and will become Mr. Wonderful until you get close, very close. This may be up to a year and beyond of dating with no recognizable signs of either abusive or controlling behavior. The red flags are subtle and so easy to explain away or be overlooked. This is a mistake.

***I can share what I now see as warnings, flags and signs.***

**1.** If you have met someone wonderful, or you are dating and falling in love, has he invited you over to his home or where he lives? I think this is so important. Is your Mr. Wonderful really living with someone else? Are there signs that someone else lives there?

If you have been dating for months, does he always come to your home and is he very comfortable there? But, has never invited you to his home? What's wrong with that? Well, he may just be following his well-rehearsed pattern and may still be living with someone else. Yes, this is a red flag. Being in someone's own environment can speak volumes of truth, so find a way to see how your love is living in his own environment.

**2.** Does he love himself or just tolerate himself? Watch for signs of self-loathing, as there may be a real reason for this. Maybe he is playing the victim or playing on your sympathy by saying, "Oh, I am so messed up." Take heed of this, if a man is in his 40s or 50s he should have figured his issues out by now, or at least be interested in some positive changes. If he is telling you he is not happy with himself or "really messed up," please do not just smile and think it's a ploy. That's is what I thought about Steven and I was so wrong. Listen and explore, see if he is willing to talk about it. If he is not pleased take this as a really bright red flag!

**3.** Does he have family? Have you met them and watched the dynamic in his family? Does he have friends? A healthy social life or outside hobbies besides drinking and partying? Is he eager to introduce you to his friends? Or does he go out with his friends as an activity that does not include you?

**4.** I do not believe in holding life choices against anyone, we are all walking our own path. For me I do not judge another but if someone has been married four, five, six times or more, chances are there is a very good reason things did not work out and chances are, you are dating the very reason why they didn't work out. So, look at past records of the person. Steven had been married six times before we met. Knowing what I know now; this was certainly a flag that was there for me to see; I just chose not to! "Silly me."

**5.** If someone has an ex (or two) how are those relationships? Do they have a relationship with their ex? Do they call them once or twice a year? Or do they call more than once a month? Is he is still calling his ex-wife multiple times during one month and is she returning all those calls? This would be a huge red flag! Why? Because it shows lack of boundaries. It shows he has no respect for his ex's new life and no concern for any one but his own ego and the need to be able to feel that no one can ever really get over him, no one can really leave. Although you become the next one in line, he still has all or at least most of his ex wives (or long-term girlfriends) in his life. This applies to both male and female ex-relationships. (In the true style of a Social Sociopath he may still be having a physical encounter or two with his ex's, regardless of their life choices or new marriages.) "Oh what a tangled web they weave."

**6.** He may have begun to not include you in meetings or dinners. Maybe letting you know he has a "business" dinner, trip, or outing. You need to know that he is not including you because he has already found new playmates. Know you are on the way out. It is hurtful when your partner shuts you out and turns away. Watch, for this will happen very subtlety, joyfully, and it will seem perfectly normal. In truth it is only normal for him.

**7.** How is your friendship? Does he really accept you for you? There is always room for improvement but how is he letting you know? Is he saying for example; "You have such beautiful hands," or is he saying "Your nails are a mess, you know people first look at your hands, go get tips or gels or something, your hands look awful"? If the undertone of someone speaking to you is abusive and controlling see it for what it is. To rationalize it as that he cares is an illusion.

**8.** Does he accept you really? Does he like the clothes you wear? Is he buying you new clothes? And, if so do you feel great in them? If he is buying you clothes that are suggestive, showing cleavage, five-inch high heels and out of your comfort zone? You may want to take a step back and think? Is his idea of beautiful really his desire to be seen with a pro? Showing you off is one thing, but dressing you up as one of his fantasy girls and going out may be a flag that, in fact, he is not really in the same reality as you are. This is easily rationalized away by thinking, "Oh, he wants me to look young and beautiful." This may be partly true but has more to do with his looking good to "have" such a prize. Please do not get caught up in thinking he cares so much. Remember what your illusion is and what may be true are two different things.

**9.** Is he being the nice guy to others and then having an irritable coldness towards you? This is verbally and emotionally abusive, and it is a controlling behavior. A big red flag! The Social Sociopath will sooner or later lose interest and consequently be irritable and sharp when he is with you. Maybe not all the time but watch for this as it is the flag that says do not walk but run to the nearest exit.

**10.** Use the Rule of three as written by Martha Stout, PhD:

"When considering a new relationship of any kind, practice the rule of three regarding the claims and promises a person makes and the responsibilities he or she has. Make the rule of three your personal policy. One lie, one broken promise, or a single neglected responsibility may be a misunderstanding instead. Two may invoke a serious mistake. But three lies says you're dealing with a liar, and deceit is the linchpin of conscienceless behavior."

Cut your losses and get out as soon as you can. Knowing what I know now, this is solid and good advice. Do not make excuses or think he just forgot or he will do it later. He did not forget and he will not do it later. After lie 347, what was I thinking?

A lie is a lie is a lie, but what if you do not know he is lying? One can only know what one knows. Be alert.

**Example:** One day Steven told me he was out in Boulder City all day. (That is about an hour away from where we lived.) The next day we were giving my friend Kathy a ride to the airport and they were talking and Steven was telling

Kathy about being at a place most of the day before that was on the other side of town ... over an hour's drive in the opposite direction from where he told me he was. I just listened and said nothing but I knew he was lying to one of us. Can you guess to whom? Listen because these lies become more and more transparent as he is halfway into his new game, and getting careless about the "game" with you.

**11.** How is his temper? Did he start out very patient? Loving everything about you? And as time goes on, is he finding fault in things and becoming nit-picky and critical? If you are living together or married, he is now relaxing into his truer colors and is quicker to verbally abuse you to yell or to be-little you or disregard you in every way you can think of. I can say from experience, for me the emotional disregard was the most challenging to deal with. This is a classic sign from a Social Sociopath that he has found a playmate or two that he now thinks suite him better. This is a flag that he may be about to complete his pattern, to throw the switch, turning your life and relationship in to a blizzard.

For many wonderful and caring women this is the time you may look at yourself and say, "What happened? What did I do?"

STOP IT! You did not bring this on in any way. This is just what happens when you get too close to someone who is carrying these traits. You know the old saying "You can't get blood from a stone?" This saying was very likely made about a "conscienceless" person. Take a deep breath and be thankful you have the ability to feel. Remember, they are searching on the outside for that which can only be found on the inside. It is about them and there is no need for you to make it any different.

**12.** How is he with you at a party? In the beginning did he stick to you like glue, wanting to be with you every moment? Did he look at you with adoring eyes as if you were really both together. Now, perhaps some time has gone by, is he still so attentive? Is he walking away and talking and drinking with others? Do you now feel as though you came to this party alone? And now, only every once in a while he will look over with a smile. Know that if this behavior persists, he is just not that into you anymore.

**13.** Conversation. Is their still stimulating conversation? Is he discussing things with you or is he telling you what you want to hear? Is he sharing with you or is he setting you up for the big fall? If he always called you a goddess each morning and now just jumps out of bed, know he is calling someone goddess … it just isn't you.

**14.** How about unusual sexual innuendoes or requests? When you are out together is he looking (hunting) for others? Is he asking you if you would like to bring her home with us? Or bring him home with us? (Yes, I am serious; this is ever-present with your social predator.)

**15.** Is he going on short trips to the store? Spending long times in the bathroom? This is a great time to be calling other women. So, when he says: "Honey I'll run and get the wine," know he is multitasking, keeping in touch with his conquests and other lovers. (Because I was getting Steven's phone bills, I was able to know the truth.) Example: One evening Steven seemed so tense and so irritable, he was in a very bad mood. So, he went and sat outside for a while. He came back in the house happy and singing … wow, what a great change! I wrote down the time in my date book and when the phone bill came I looked at that time and sure enough he went outside and had a nice long conversation with one of his Canadian loves. And here I thought it was my winning personality!

**16.** These days a background check is not out of the question. You may have met Mr. Wonderful by accident but, make no mistake, if you fit the profile of what he missed in infancy you will be deliberately hunted, charmed, captured, and eventually destroyed, or as close to it as he can come. (His father may have been over-the-top controlling or brutal. His mother may have been an executive or had little or no emotional attachment with Mr. Wonderful. He will unconsciously be hunting for a woman who is independent, has a business or seen as successful and has a certain flair and a kind and nurturing side as well.) If you fit that description be extra careful out there. Do a background check. Some even say, if you know of his ex's, contact them and find out why the relationship ended, from their point of view, not his.

**17.** Is your love blowing up at every little thing? Anthony would react disproportionately to situations. He would explode over a situation that had not even happened yet; he would be thinking about what "might" take place, and he would work himself into a rage. Watch for this verbally abusive behavior, yes it is like a spoiled child and also a red flag.

**18.** Every social sociopath is different in their behavior and yet will have some traits that may resemble other social sociopaths. Does your guy or gal have a chip on their shoulder?

A sense of entitlement? What happens when they do not get their own way? Do they brood? Get angry? Or use punishing techniques? Like not speaking to you, or being rough with you verbally, emotionally, mentally, or physically? Do they become the bully? This is a red flag.

**19.** Max was the life of the party. so Is your love the life of the party, funny and charming, and very popular? Take a step back and observe a bit deeper. Does he or she keep his or her word? Are they honest? Do they have integrity? Does he or she stick to the same story or does it change depending on to whom he or she is speaking? And does he or she support you? Encourage you to join in, listen when you speak, show you respect?

**20.** Is your love always trying to convince you to do something you don't feel comfortable doing? If so, you have a master manipulator on your hands. Not all charming fun people are sociopaths, but most Social Sociopaths are fun and charming, and they are all master manipulators! Max was the greatest at getting Terra to do things that she was just not comfortable with. Terra stated that she often felt used or like a toy. All that mattered is what Max wanted, there was little regard for how she felt about it.

Remember, the only way to stop any abuse – verbal, emotional, physical, or controlling behavior – is to stop! The only way to stop is to STOP!

*"Awareness is the first step towards change"*

**SZS**

# CHAPTER 13

---

# Why and How
# Do They Get Away With It?

Because we let them! A man who has five or six women or more at a time is applauded in our society. He is embraced as the top of his food chain. He juggles people like a clown juggles bowling pins. Everyone keeps the secrets, including me. For those astute enough to see the rage just underneath the surface of these creatures, everyone walks on eggshells being sure to please the sociopath after all he's such a nice guy, yes, he may drink too much and sometimes is sexually inappropriate but everybody loves him so, he must be okay. I myself used this reasoning in the beginning. I thought, "Steven had been in a 14-year marriage, so he must be okay."

Please do not assume that just because someone has been married they are suitable for a relationship. Look at the warning signs and if friends try and warn you, take heed. I rationalized that he must have grown up and matured, to be so devastated in his last break up. I was among the masses who thought a sociopath is a criminal and most are behind bars. There is no law for breaking hearts and homes. No law against shattered dreams and emotional cruelty, no laws against deliberate devastation, so, buyer beware. These predators are out there and in a constant search for their next "game" or "victim."

# CHAPTER 14

---

# The Research...
# Finding the Truth

I'll admit that at the time I was beginning this research, I was close to the edge in many ways. Realizing I was living with a real live "Social Sociopath" and what's more I was in love with him. How was that possible? Being a well-educated woman, published author, a sincere person who speaks out about injustices, a woman who loves and honors all life … how was this possible? In my professional life I teach health and wellness, including an all day intensive workshop on "Unraveling Patterns" and living a joyful and fulfilled life. And yet here I was living in chaos, confusion, sorrow, and an unwillingness to believe that almost every word spoken to me by my "partner" was a lie.

I had so many questions for myself. How did I not see this? And now living together for over two years, tangled up financially, emotionally (my side of course) mentally and physically I didn't know what to do. I am smart, loving, genuine, giving, and well-respected in the community. Well, I am here to let you know it can happen to anyone! There are no signs. They are charming, charismatic, and seem to be so caring, and generous! From a distance they look like a perfect mate, right! Wrong! (Refer to "Ring of Fire." Chapter 17)

Being an author and always doing my due diligence, I really began to do research on this topic of sociopathic behaviors. I read many books on this subject and was surprised to find so many books on the topic. It really did help me to know that "I am not so crazy, this is really happening!" Most of the books I read were from a perspective of clinical physiatrists and not from inside exposure.

During my research, I read two of the four books written by best selling author, Patricia Evans. The Verbally Abusive Relationship and Controlling People. After reading them, I wanted even more insight, so I actually called Patricia for a consultation. She was very gracious and we had a long conversation that helped make things crystal clear for me.

Patricia explained that when a male is carrying these traits, she refers to him as the abuser. It is almost always due to a father that is either absent, controlling or emotionally unavailable. As a result, there is a part of the child that is not realized, like a lost part of the personality. When he establishes a relationship this lost self (sometimes called his "feminine side") is projected into his partner. The abuser then feels irritated or attacked when the partner doesn't act like his projection. Patricia also said, "If his mother didn't express love toward him, or was not emotionally available to him, then he is likely doubly damaged."

This view seems to explain the behavior. However, some psychologists look at the nature (genetic) vs. nurture (how he was treated) debate and question whether an abusive childhood can create an abusive adult. Some only consider physical abuse in arriving at their conclusions so miss the impact of rejection, disparagement, or rage directed at the child.

Patricia shared with me how this behavior could be seen as a quest for the lost part of the personality. The warm, receptive, emotionally intelligent self. Steven fell in love with me, he saw me through the vision of his lost self – all warmth and love, everything he wanted ... the missing rest of himself. Once he felt secure that he had me he projected that lost self into me. However, I did not match his projection, so anything I said or did was, to him, irritating or attacking. He was angry even though there was no conflict. So, the switch was flipped on, and out he went as he has always done, going on to the next woman, still looking for the "missing piece," and attracted to women whose appearance appeals to him. "They are all possible partners in his quest to feel connected within and to the world."

Patricia said, "Some men consequently seek sex with many women and yet seem never satisfied. Whether he is single, married or living with someone in a committed relationship has no bearing on his behavior. I know it sounds impossible but it is true."

Patricia further explained, "People with these traits do not know how to truly connect with people and do not look at their chosen one as a person. They do not see or realize that they do not look at women as people, rather as objects and toys." (This hit home for me as even in the beginning if Steven was to rough with me he would say, "Ohhh, did I break my toy?").

Patricia said, "Yes, he seems to seek many women, needing back ups for his back ups." She thought it was amazing that we were living together for more than two years when I saw what he was doing. I told her that he knew that I knew, and that I had been getting the phone bills for over a year, just so I could have some idea of the truth. Social Sociopaths are driven by their infancy needs. "They are driven to get their lost self back."

I asked about his dislike for anything out of order. Patricia shared that those who have these traits must have order around them. Driven to establish order out of the chaos of their childhoods and that they don't realize why they behave as they do.

Patricia shared that he does not get that I am a person but a symbol. Not capable of a real relationship. They want what is missing, they want their lost self, and they want and want.

They are usually very smart and highly manipulative and release rage when having sex.

I recommend picking up and reading Patricia's bestsellers *The Verbally Abusive Relationship* and *Controlling People.* These are real eye openers!

The Social Sociopath will have control issues and most will certainly be passive aggressive with verbal abuse and this can grow into full-blown mental, emotional, and physical abuse as time goes on.

Some of the characteristics of verbal abuse were such an eye opener I list them below. From Patricia Evans:

"All the patients I interviewed had heard two or more of the following declarations of love. Some very abusive men had frequently said them all. Verbal abusers have been known to say, "I love you, no one could love you as much as I do, I'd never leave you, I'd never do anything to hurt you, and I just want you to be happy." (My Social Sociopath said four out of the five.) It is abuse because it is a lie.

Another National Best seller is *"The Sociopath Next Door"* by Martha Stout PhD.

She takes a hard stand and on the cover it says, "Who is the devil you know?" I would like to put a few details in from this author, but my views are not as drastic. Perhaps they should be, but my heart says different. She would probably refer to me as being "clinically traumatized" and I would agree with her. Nonetheless, she says, " What distinguishes all of these people from the rest of us is an utterly empty hole in the psyche where there should be the most evolved of all humanizing functions. The inner mechanism that beats up on us, emotionally speaking when we make a choice we view as immoral, unethical, neglectful, or selfish. Most of us feel mildly guilty if we eat the last piece of cake in the kitchen, let alone what we would feel if we intentionally and methodically set about to hurt another person. Those who have no conscience at all are a group unto themselves, whether they be homicidal tyrants or merely ruthless social snipers." As drastic as this sounds, I do agree with her.

I was amazed there was so much information on this. We

are not alone! As our society has become more and more career oriented, the real fall-out are the children who have no emotional attachment to their mothers and no emotional attachment to life other than their own. Many fathers are gone most of the time and some are controlling and overbearing and angry themselves. There are other causes as well, some scientist say it can be environmental or even genetic. Most physiologists believe you cannot work with, improve, or get beyond this behavior. I want to believe differently, but then again I believe anything is possible and now that I think of it, that is probably one of the traits that attracted Steven to me, and one that caused me to believe the illusion. There is a good reason that this behavior was once called " moral insanity."

# CHAPTER 15

---

# Facts and Fictions

**Fact:** 1 in every 25 adults in this country has Sociopathic behavior.

**Fact:** That is about 4% of the population. And the majority of adults carrying this behavior are male.

**Fiction:** "It's not so bad. Some of the relationship is good."

**Fact:** This kind of mental and emotional abuse is TOXIC to you.

**Fact:** "He is such a neat freak."

He demands order because inconsistency "chaos" or a messy room brings up "inner chaos" from childhood and infancy.

**Fiction:** He doesn't realize he is this way.

"Straight from the horses mouth." When I asked Steven if he knew the difference between a lie and the truth, he answered; "Yes, I do." Then I asked, "So you do this deliberately?" He looked at me raised his eyebrows and shook his head in a great big Yes!

**Fiction:**  They can change:

Just get over it; these people are the most selfish people on the planet. They look normal and seem to be so giving on the outside. Since they think they are superior and the master of the game there is a slim to none chance of change for the better.

**Fact:**  You may not be able to identify or see any "flags" until the switch is flexed and that will be way too late. (There is a time when it is like a switch is flipped   and the behavior of the  Social Sociopath is pushed to the next level of the traits.) That is what I refer to as a flexed switch.

**Fact:**  They give up quality for quantity, ever searching on the outside for that which is missing on the inside.

**Fiction:**  These are caring people that just are misunderstood.

**Fact:**  These are man/boys that are spoiled and must have  their own way and instant gratification or things can get ugly.

**Fact:**  Many unconsciously or consciously will punish you if you do not give them their own way. Like a spoiled child they may quit talking to you, may brood, and be a bully of sorts, may get mean and distant until they either forget about it or you become or do what they want.

# CHAPTER 16

---

# The Real Solution: What To Do & Words of Wisdom

The truth is the real solution lies within you. It is not so much about what has happened to us but how we handle these events and what we come away with. When we encounter "catalysts" in our lives; it is up to us to uncover the blessings they bring. Your life is seen uniquely through your eyes, your own perception of what life is for you. Each of us has a long history of thoughts, feelings, and experiences that define how and what we perceive. You hold, we each hold, a unique and special place on this planet, therefore it is our responsibility to experience, work on, and raise the consciousness of the one person that can change our world, enhance our life experience and bring joy, inspiration and peace to our lives. That person is you! It is I; it is every single one of us knowing that we are responsible for our life experiences.

When we experience what some people might consider disasters in our lives it is up to us to uncover the positive, the reason we experienced it and how we are better for it. To grow into the good of the experience and allow the rest to fall away like dried leaves falling from the autumn tree. In the end the choice is entirely up to us how we choose to view this encounter with one of these beautiful, playful, dangerous, and deadly creatures.

Is there recovery time? Yes. Is there a process of bewilderment, sorrow, sense of loss, and aloneness? Yes. Is there anger and feelings of grief? Yes. Disappointment and isolation? Yes! These all take some time to work through. But work through them you must. Feel as bad as you feel, embrace your sorrow, love it, and nurture yourself. You will come through a wiser person, who is empowered in your own self-love and self-understanding. When you can feel truly grateful for the experience then you know you have come through and are better for it.

For me, I am grateful for the good that came out of my relationship with a Social Sociopath; the smiles and laughter, the love and caring. Because for me it was real and I choose to allow the hurt, the pain, the disappointment, and the pulling on my heart to fall away, to cease the draining of my precious energy, to finally be gone from my thoughts and my being. I embrace the event and let it go, I choose to have a joyous life, I believe and see having a joyous and inspired life, and so it is.

## What to do:

**1.** Get to know your gut instinct. That feeling something may not be just right. This is your own body telling you "something is wrong."

**2.** Pay attention, the goal of the Social Sociopath when in a social setting is to receive attention. Just don't go there.

**3.** Don't take the bait. His charming ways are to entice

you into playing his game. This will be the first step in his controlling, conquering and destroying game plan.

**4.** Do your homework. Get to know all about him or her. Not all men are narcissist or a Social Sociopath but many are, so go slow and recognize the red flags before you even have your first kiss.

**5.** Do not give up your friends or your life. If you seem to becoming more and more isolated and your mate seems to want to be your whole world, remember... you have a life and friends as well. Your friends are like beautiful flowers in your garden; enjoy them and keep them near.

**6.** Remember, sociopaths are masters of subtly. You really have to be paying attention and living in the here and now to realize who and what they are. Denial is one of the best weapons in a sociopath's arsenal – YOUR denial. Because they are so sweet and charming and fun you tell yourself you're imaging these little innuendos. You pretend that you didn't notice some irregularity justifying it like; "well, he's just really tired" or "he'll do it later." At first, these occurrences happen maybe once every few months. But they add up and become more and more frequent. Every couple of weeks and then weekly. The sociopath is less careful the longer he or she has been with you. Trust your instincts. If something feels wrong it probably is.

**7.** If the people truly close to you (parents, relatives, best friends) are uncomfortable with your new love, listen to them. They can see things as they truly are. One of Terra's two best friends to this day says she loved Max, but everyone else – her brothers included – didn't want her to marry him.

They supported Terra's decision but it was not their choice for her. (That girlfriend who loved Max has been through a string of tough marriages herself.)

Terra's mistake in her relationship with Max was ignoring all of the tiny warnings sent to her. They were small but enough that if she had a few more facts and paid attention she may have made different choices. She told me, "The night before our wedding I did not sleep one second. I spent the entire night trying to figure out how to get out of it! I kept telling myself it was just the jitters. After my divorce I said this to my dad and he was like 'OMG! If we had known there's no way we would have let you go through it! We could see who he was.' Remember to ask your family and trusted friends, and listen to what they have to say. Sometimes they can see clearer from a distance.

# CHAPTER 17

# The Ring of Fire

Like fire, if you keep your distance it brings warmth and that wonderful cozy feeling. Come a bit closer and sometimes it can mesmerize you, draw you in until your cheeks are hot and you must back away. But to stand in the fire is torturous pain, it means slow and horrible mode of destruction.
The same holds true for social contact with a sociopath.
To be in love and in relationship with a sociopath is to stand in the fire.

## A "Relationship"

A Social Sociopath is in a relationship with him or herself, so saying the word or using the word "relationship" in the same sentence or in reference to someone who carries this trait or pattern is an oxymoron. The very word relationship refers to an exchange of feeling, caring, and emotion between two people. A Social Sociopath has "Emotional Detachment" the opposite of the ability to have a relationship.

To be friends or fun buddies or surface friends is to be in the happy zone, you will have a great time and everything will seem so perfect. To be in love or in "relation" with a Social Sociopath is to stand in the fire.

# The Ring of Fire

**Level 1:**
"In the Fire" Disappointment, devistation, heartbreak and shattered dreams. This is the object of his desire, the relationship or marriage.

**Level 2:**
You may see some clues that something is not quite right. An angry outburst or catch a glimps of a lie or self serving fantasy.

**Level 3** is the outer ring. This is a great place to be as you are far from the pattern, and the wearer of the pattern may seem to be the most charming, intelligent and fun person to be around. This is safe for most all. To be a casual friend or employer, remaining on the outside regardless of how well you think you know him or her.

## *Lets look at the three zones:*
## ZONE 3

The outer realms of the Sociopath.
*(This is where you want to remain.)*
Zone 3 is rated G and safe for all.

The three rings are much like a fire. If you stay a distance from it, it is warm and comforting' it feels wonderful on a cold night.

When you meet a "Steven, Anthony, Max or a Ted" you feel warm and wonderful; they are charismatic and charming, generous to a fault. A wonderful conversationalist will always make you feel so special, loved and cared for. He is kind and patient as long as it's all fun and games. He opens the door for you and appears to be the perfect gentleman.

If you are an acquaintance or a work colleague you will have to admit his creative flare and seemingly high intelligence, loyal to his work or at least will keep the appearance of being loyal to his work. In fact, he may choose to stay busy with projects as this gives him the "game board" in which he can unfold the pattern. Remember, you are safe and warm and feel wonderful as long as you remain in Zone 3 you will not see and are not likely to experience any of the sociopathic behavior. Zone 3 is the place to be.

## ZONE 2

**Zone 2 is rated GX and may not be so safe.**
If you are working with or casually dating and even having a physical fling with a Social Sociopath, you may be in no

danger unless he is intrigued by you. You will know if he is hunting you by the intenseness of his attention. If you get to know him or her better some rage may slip out in the form of yelling at you or being short and brutal for a moment. Then he or she will come back all better as if nothing at all has happened. A worker once said to me, "I have seen the other side of my boss." He said he was shocked, as it was scary and cold. All I could say was just wear a smile and keep things light and you'll be okay. Do not push him or expect any slack from him. He thanked me for the insight and that was that.

Zone 2 can be a fun place, as you will be going to more events but beware because this is the zone that he will decide what to do next. If you are lucky he will enjoy you and then tell you "I'm Done" and move on. It may be shocking and a bit hurtful but, so much safer than the fire. Be grateful for the fun and games and know that your sociopath is a hollow shell, do not expect emotional attachment or true caring. They are not able to experience that and if it feels like that then you are already in the illusion. Run, run like your life depends on it.

Real relationships grow and change; they ripen and mature, as you become better and deeper friends and lovers with your mate, your partner. The feeling deepens and so does your love and understanding for each other. This is the opposite of what happens when you are in "relation" with a person who carries the traits of a "Social Sociopath" a conscious-less person. They grow away and distant, revealing more of their shallow self the longer you are near them. The change from deep to shallow is not the desired change for a true love or someone who has true feelings.

# ZONE 1
## Zone 1 is rated XXX  (the Fire)
Do not go here! Danger, Danger!
Be smart with your heart, Have great discernment.

They say it is better to love and loose than to not love at all.  Well, if you love someone, do your homework first; make sure he or she has a heart and not just a long trail of tragedies.

So you have been dating for a long while maybe even a full year, you have no idea about his "secret life" at this time, and no idea his heart is made of steel or worse yet, hollow. He has been so careful to show you the very best of what he knows, the best of his game, kind and caring, helpful and generous. Always holding your hand and holding you, peering into your eyes and saying how much he loves you. You are in attention heaven and in love with all its awesome splendor. As time moves forward you notice that your wonderful conversations have all but disappeared. In it place is surface talk. Now and again you catch a glimpse of irritation, a far away look, and the realization comes that now you are living together and have made a relationship. Your mate seems less and less interested in love and more interested in sex, and perhaps sometimes with a twist.  At a time when a relationship is usually deepening, somehow this relationship seems to be getting shallower. You were such close friends and now he begins to treat you as if you are a stranger. (This would be a good time to see if he is willing to talk about it. Take note of his reaction and take his reaction to heart.)

When you conform to his specifications, he is wonderful, and when you do not, he is becomes agitated. More and more what would become a deeper love is now becoming shallow and superficial.

*Let me pause here and ask:* **What are your expectations?**

What is your expectation of love? Is it respectful? Kind? Understanding? Is it stimulating to your mind, body, and spirit? Is it a walk on the beach, a caress when you feel low? Is it someone to hold you when you are sad and some one to rejoice with you when you are glad? Is it a friendship that will go beyond time, enhance your life as you co-create the sublime? Know your own heart and know what love is in your eyes, it is less easy to be led down the path that ends in the fire.

Let's say some information comes to you and you explore it, finding that this wonderful man has never stopped all his other affairs, or is in the midst of new affairs. You find out he is having serious relations with many others. That means long conversations, dating, sleeping, loving these women just as he is doing with you. You realize he is careless and will have sex with anything that walks, no condoms and that puts everyone at risk. Each one knows nothing of the others. The behavior begins to make perfect sense as you go day to day in a loveless relationship. He makes all the right moves but you can now see they are moves. When away he calls but only wants to talk for a minute. He is always in a hurry. You are being slowly taken down, the little remarks and the non-approval, you can see he is doing everything to destroy what he "says" he wants. At this point the ball is in your hands, I know you want to believe you were different and the fact is he did probably love you at one point to the best of his sociopathic ability. But now you remind him of his chaos and drama. You remind him that with love comes responsibility and he wants no part of that. It is torture to be with some one who has no conscience, feels no remorse, no feeling of any kind about what he is doing or how it may be affecting others.

It is now your choice to stay in the illusion of what once was a great love. I remember saying to Steven, "You have devastated so many women, probably a dozen just since we have been living together; what are you doing? What kind of legacy are you leaving? You get these women to fall in love with you and then you are "done."

Let me be clear, if your partner is carrying sociopathic traits he was most likely this way long before he met you and this behavior has been going on secretly since you have been together. If a bit of anger or irritation is showing it is only a matter of time before he flips (or flexes) the switch on you and moves on to his next conquest.

Expect no kindness, no hint of responsibility or remorse; when he is done he is done and you are now viewed as the enemy, the one who reminds him of disappointment and his spoiled attempt to once again feel love. This was hardest part of all for me. If you stand in this fire expect to be burned. He will not feel complete unless you are emotionally vaporized, cremated, and blown away. He will be gone long before he leaves and the illusion becomes only to clear. Stay out of the fire.

LOVE & ILLUSION

# CHAPTER 18

---

# Being Grateful in
# The Face of Disaster

So, how do you find that place of being grateful when you are heart broken, angry, upset, and your life feels like it is in a mess? Maybe it was a week, a few months, or a few years that you were close to someone who carries some of the these traits we have discussed. All you know is your life as you knew it is gone. All the "I love you's" meant nothing. Well, perhaps at the moment they were said it was true in that moment, but maybe not. It is not up to us to figure it out now, only to be grateful the lies and the illusion has ended. If he or she was brutal to you in any way, this too has ended. No more deceit and games, no more coming home with love in your heart only to be met with a brooding child or worse, an angry bully.

If all things are in divine timing than this is your time to look at the situation in a different light. Yes, you need the time to grieve, to be angry, not with yourself but perhaps the situation. Because we are real women and men who love. Yes, our heart may be broken but remember your spirit is vibrant, your heart is brilliant and true, this sorrow and chaos will dwindle and peace will return to you in time. Have you looked at the situation in a way that shows you all the wonderful times you experienced? Can you find a way to feel the love and the joy you felt and hang on to that? Not for him or her but for yourself. This will pass and you will love again, emerging a smarter and wiser human being.

Search for things to be grateful for, they are there. How have you grown? What new inspirations do you have? You have been given the gift of yourself and the time now to explore the wondrous and magnificent being you are. Be grateful you are now the one loving yourself and allowing yourself to heal and be free from the chaos and drama.

### Here is an example of being grateful even in the face of disaster:

When Steven came into my life my home was a bit messy, I was lax about my hair and nails. In the beginning he helped me to see the places of clutter and they were cleaned up. Steven was so happy and grateful just to be with me. But, after a while his subtle verbal abuse began. He started making comments about the rooms, my hair, my nails, and my cloths even though my home was now free from clutter and my hair and nails were being professionally done, nothing seemed to be just good enough to please him. This behavior tried to tear me down and I am grateful to be away from the quiet abuse and the critical eye. Steven was so generous. He loved buying me cloths and dressing me up to look how he wanted me to look. Most of the time it was great. But wearing five-inch spikes and showing allot of cleavage was Steven's fantasy, not mine.

I am so grateful to be wearing what makes me feel comfortable. Not feeling like I have to sleep in my make up and wear boots or spikes all the time. I am so grateful for all the beautiful gifts and yes I will miss that but I am grateful for having the experience. I am grateful for the months of wonderful love (even though it was just a game for him, it was real for me). I am even grateful for me holding on to the illusion when the reality was just too much to deal with. It is your turn to be grateful for all these things and more.

Be grateful for your beautiful heart and the ability to love and be giving. Grateful you have come through a wiser being. Grateful you have found and nurtured your own heart. Go into the sunlight and feel true warmth from the universe. You are a beautiful being and your next love will be real.

Being grateful is a high vibration and we need not lower our own state of being by feeling angry, jealous or envious or any of the negative feelings that can crop up. Just hold on to the good and let the rest go. The disaster has hit and no amount of fussing will put it back together. And knowing what you now know, be grateful for the ending and a new beginning for yourself. Every day, even though you are so disappointed and sad, remember how wonderful it is to have your life back, to live in truth and feel the sunlight on your soul again. Be kind to yourself, do nice things for yourself. Know that his pattern will go on and on but you will find true love, be grateful, be grateful. Yes, be grateful and watch as the disaster turns to a bright new day for you.

*"The best revenge is to live well"*

# CHAPTER 19

---

# Resolution and Recovery

When does that time come? We can tell ourselves, "Things are not so bad; sometimes there are wonderful moments." (There is your clue.) When the wonderful times seem like moments and the pain and anguish of living or loving a liar, a cheat, and some one who only respects their own desires and has no regard for you or yours takes hold, resolve yourself to love yourself and get out. If the pattern has gotten advanced and you have fear of the rage that lies just beneath the surface, get out carefully. Since a Social Sociopath seeks to destroy their own happiness and the happiness of their current mate, getting out may not be a problem. Your own emotion and bewilderment of what has happened to your life might be more of an issue. For those of us who truly love, we feel the pain of separation and with the knowledge that you really were a game and mean nothing to the person you have been loving and living with there comes a flooding of feeling and a sort of disbelief of where you allowed your self to be.

## On Recovery:
If you are in a close relation with a Social Sociopath or know of one, you need to know that there is no greater mental, emotional, or verbal abuse than the unconscious (or conscious) behavior of a Social Sociopath.

Know with certainty this will NOT get better, it is an illusion to think or believe one day he or she will wake up. He or she cannot. That tiny mechanism that allows us to be human, to truly feel, to truly love is broken and kept tucked away in the unconscious of the person carrying these traits. Get out before the destruction is complete, they will walk away anyway, save yourself, and break the spell. Tear free from the illusion and the lies. Love yourself enough to bring real life back into you life.

The sooner you begin the process of taking care of yourself the sooner the spell will be broken. The illusion will turn to reality. It takes time. For me, I am mindful to be grateful for every moment.

Yes, grateful to be out from under emotional, mental, verbal abuse, of course. But also grateful for the moments of joy and the wonder that love brings because for me it was real. Even though the devastating disappointment and knowing he "switched" two weeks before Christmas so as to inflict the maximum injury, I could feel the desire to warn his new "love." She is a single woman raising two boys, and I know she has no clue who I am, and no idea what is in store for her as Steven reins her in … as he did me … and so many others.

Know that being thankful for surviving and having the courage to say "ENOUGH" is huge.

The most important component in recovery is to have a good support system. Friends and family who know what you have been going through and will be there for you every day for a while. This is key. You must not keep this a secret. John Bradshaw once said, "You are only as sick as your secrets," and this is true. Tell somebody, maybe a few friends and family, allow them to be a support for you. Yes, they will get sick of hearing about it but it is a path back to reality. Knowing the consequences of a close relationship with one of these predator's will help you to see and know to look deep before you leap the next time. Remember to breathe, and know you are a wonderful person and yes, even though your heart is breaking, be thankful you have the ability and the blessing to feel. Remember, you are the lucky one for you will love again and your Social Sociopath will only continue the endless and empty hunt for that piece that is missing but cannot be found.

Get ready for the recovery because, you had no idea it was such a long way back. You did not even realize how you became more and more isolated. This incredible flower with the deadly nectar will leave and there will be an empty space in your heart and in your home and in your life. The feelings of loss and aloneness will be overwhelming (even though you knew it was coming). It will be overwhelming because you have a heart and you really gave your all and you really thought it was real. So you have been thrown into a black hole of empty words and embraces that felt so real you melted into them and yes, you believed the lies. You surrendered to love as it turned to cold stone. Get ready to feel it all and do not think for a moment there will be caring or kindness coming from him or her, for he has moved on even before he left. Moved on long ago; he who has no responsibility or conscience, no remorse or guilt. He even thinks he is the victim and you are to blame! Get ready for the reality that you have been living an illusion, a hollow lie, unknowingly playing his game. When he is done he is done. Steven once said to me "You'll be the last to know." I did not want to be the last to know, so, I got the phone bills and it was a real eye opener. The quiet control and sometimes not so quiet control of a sociopathic person will have you isolated as they maneuver themselves to get ready for the kill. They demand to be your everything, and when they feel this has been accomplished the game is over.

The good news is you are not alone; your support of loving friends and family will help to see you through. Be thankful for breaking free from the drama and chaos, be thankful for separating yourself from the quiet abuse and maybe not so quiet abuse. Know you have a heart and were really a caring, supportive and loving person, mate or partner. Time will help to heal you. Get out and do the things that help you to laugh and smile. Yes, there will be an empty place where your feelings of love and belonging used to be, known that they will be filled again. Work on your own life and your own blooming, take a class, paint, hike, meet new people and be grateful you survived this ordeal.

One early afternoon when having lunch with an attorney friend of mine, we began to talk about this writing and he shared with me that he himself had been through the devastation with a female Social Sociopath. He had some words of wisdom I would like to share with you:

He said: "In reference to my own wrenching relationship experience, after it was finally all over the one thing I really kick myself about is that I let my hurt and anger go on way,

way too long. I now know why. It was the only way I had left to hang on to at least a piece of her and I just didn't want to let completely go. But, it's sick and it's nothing but negative vibe for the person who hangs on. And such a tragic waste of time. If you want to be whole again you have to will yourself to let go, and then move on." This is a true statement.

*"Happiness is when - what you think, what you say, and what you do are in harmony"*

Mahatma Gandhi

# CHAPTER 20

---

# Good Advice &
# Heartfelt Wisdom

Know that this charmer can be anywhere, know that you are not different from anyone else, know he will seek and destroy your heart if you get to close.

These Social Sociopaths are great to dine with and have fun with. Know you are on sinking sand if you allow yourself to fall for them.

Love yourself, love yourself, keep your distance from the fire or you will get burned.

I want to hang on to hope there are real men out there, with real hearts and real feelings and who have the ability and capacity to love.

What do you do with a shattered heart, shattered home, broken dreams and promises?

For me, I dust myself off, hold on to my precious heart and vibrant spirit and write a long over due book to help the hundreds maybe 1,000s of hearts that have come in contact with what some therapists consider pure evil. I would like to think in God's eyes they are NOT evil but lost and angry at the world and themselves. "They destroy all who come close enough to make them feel."

I have made my stand, I will not be devastated, and I will see my dreams unfold before me. I am wiser now, and I share what I have experienced and learned with you. Because you are a beautiful soul. Live in truth, live in integrity. Laugh every day and feel the sunlight upon you. Love truly and do your homework. It's a new day and our eyes are wide open.

# Epilogue

Go into the world equipped with wisdom and discernment. Know as you move from healing to true joy you will be able to see the blessings in all things and be able to feel grateful for every moment, every encounter. You now know the truth and the truth will set you free. Yes, be firmly planted in reality and actuality, one who knows the truth, knows the danger to you, your heart, your mind, your spirit and your soul. One who knows you deserve to be loved and cherished. One who knows how much we all want to be loved and cherished.

So, be aware there are wolves in sheep's clothing out there. They are charming and charismatic people who do mean you harm. They will pursue you for the hunt and the game.

Flee, flee fast and know there are good people who will love you without killing you.

Share this book, teach your young ones and your grandmothers because age, social status, geographic boundaries will not keep you from harms way.

My mother once said to me, "If something feels like it is to good to be true it probably is"

May the force be with you,
Sheila Z Stirling Ph.D.

# Last word

To my Social Sociopath, I want you to know when you stayed in the hospital with me for three days; it caused me to believe in you as a wonderful, caring human being. You stretched your boundaries in being there for me. In my eyes it was heroic and I will remember the spark of grace I saw in you those three days. It does not make your behavior acceptable on any level; it does not excuse your heartless actions and blizzard ways. It does not excuse your total disregard and disrespect for me and our life together; it does not excuse you not taking responsibility for your actions, your lies and your cruelty.

But know I will always think of those three days as having a glimpse of the grace you once held, the real human you could have been and I will pray for you and hold that time dear to me. Just wanted you to know.

Through this time with you I have soared to incredible highs only to lie lifeless, tired and bewildered, with my heart and dreams shattered. You have stretched my human experience and for that I am grateful.

I am not conquerable. I am not permanently breakable. The cruelty, brutality, lies and self-serving behavior only destroys the weaker and honey, that means you.

And to all you wonderful, kind, and nurturing women who are open to real love: Know that you deserve to smile, deserve to laugh and to be loved, to feel joy and warmth of a true embrace. You deserve the truth on every level, you deserve to be respected and honored. You deserve all the best life has to offer. So please remember "what does not bring you joy is too small for you." Keep your eyes open and fill them with beauty and true love, it does exist and it is out there for you.

Be wise, be yourself, be happy.
Not the End But a New Beginning

About the Author:
Sheila Z Stirling, Ph. D has authored books, CDs and workshops on the cutting edge of health and wellness. She now shares her personal experience, backed up with science and research on this chilling subject.

I would like to hear your story.
Please submit to:
True Life Solutions
4132 S Rainbow Blvd. #465
Las Vegas, NV 89103

# Index of information

Social Sociopath - This is a term created by Sheila Z Stirling that describes the behavior of the Sociopath that has learned to use their emotional detachment and rage to their advantage. They live among us, sometimes barely within the boundries of society.

Patricia Evans - Author of The Verbally Abusive Relationship, Controlling People and Survivors Speak Out – interpersonal communications specialist and the author of five books on the topic of verbal abuse. www.patriciaevans.com

Martha Stout, PhD: Do not join the game. Intrigue is a sociopath's tool. Resist the temptation to compete with a seductive sociopath, to outsmart him, psychoanalyze, or even banter with him. In addition to reducing yourself to his level, you would be distracting yourself from what is really important, which is to protect yourself. www.bookbrowse.com/author_interviews/full/index.cfm?author_number=1097

www.hare.org

(Lisa E Scott – It's All About Him) http://www.lisaescott.com/forum/2010/01/27/12-characteristics-psychopaths-sociopaths

http://abcnews.go.com/GMA/video/joran-van-der-sloot-confesses-murder-10853717.

Quote from "Intentional Wellness" Create your optimal life now. By Sheila Z Stirling: http://www.openwisdominstitute.com/esales/catalog.html. "Each one of us has a long history of thoughts, feelings and experiences that define how and what we perceive"

www.medicinenet.com/sexual_addiction/article.htm - Article and facts on Sexual Addiction.

Question on sexual Addiction: www.sexhelp.com/sast.cfm

www.sexaddict.com/ - A counseling Center for Sexual Addiction.

Wikipedia:
Malignant narcissism is a syndrome consisting of a combination of aspects of narcissistic personality disorder and antisocial personality disorder as well as paranoid traits. Malignant narcissism should be considered a theoretical or 'experimental' diagnostic category; although narcissistic personality disorder is found in the current version of the Diagnostic and Statistical Manual of Mental Disorders (DSM-IV-TR), malignant narcissism is not. Individuals with malignant narcissism would be diagnosed under narcissistic personality disorder. Malignant narcissism can be partially treated with medications and therapy helping to reduce aggravating symptoms.

The malignant narcissist differs from narcissistic personality disorder in that the malignant narcissist derives higher levels of psychological gratification from accomplishments over time (thus worsening the disorder). Because the malignant narcissist becomes more involved in this psychological gratification, they are apt to develop the antisocial, the paranoid, and the schizoid personality disorders. The term malignant is added to the term narcissist to indicate that individuals with this disorder tend to worsen in their impulse controls and desires over time.
http://www.sociopathworld.com/2009/04/sociopaths-narcissistic-not-narcissists.html   (difference between narcissist. And sociopathic)

http://www.lovefraud.com/blog/2007/05/11/ask-dr-leedom-what-is-the-difference-between-a-narcissist-and-a-sociopath/ (difference between nar. And soc)

Wikipedia:
Psychopathy is a personality disorder characterized by an abnormal lack of empathy combined with strongly amoral conduct, masked by an ability to appear outwardly normal. Neither psychopathy, nor the similar concept of sociopathy, are nowadays defined in international diagnostic manuals, which instead describe a category of antisocial/

dissocial personality disorder. However, researcher Robert Hare, whose Hare Psychopathy Checklist is widely used, describes psychopaths as "interspecies predators" as does R.I. Simon. Elsewhere Hare and others write that psychopaths "use charisma, manipulation, intimidation, sexual intercourse and violence" to control others and to satisfy their own needs. Hare states that: "Lacking in conscience and empathy, they take what they want and do as they please, violating social norms and expectations without guilt or remorse." He previously stated that: "What is missing, in other words, are the very qualities that allow a human being to live in social harmony."

## Also by Sheila Z. Stirling:

### Intentional Wellness
*Creating your Optimal Life Now*

*"Now and then someone comes along who demonstrates deep insight into the dynamics of reality. Sheila Z Stirling is one of those people stated.* – Dr. Vernon Woolf Ph.D."

The Intentional Wellness Book serves as the road map and the workbook that explains the all day workshop of the same name. The place where tools for a successful life can be gained. The key to unlocking emotional health and well being that is a crucial piece in our life success.

Available at: wisdompresspublishing.com
www.truelife-solutions.com

$19.95 plus $4 shipping within the United States.
Also available at Amazon.com and Barns and Noble.com
For more information call 866-612-7051

## Also by Sheila Z. Stirling:

### Reading the Language of the Cosmos

2010 Astrology Guide

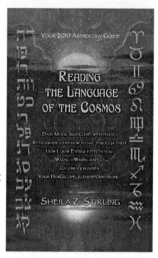

This is a full Astrology guide and so much more. It is unique as it speaks about the energy of the Cosmos. This yearly Almanac has a daily moon chart that explains the incoming energies and how they effect your every day life.

"A rare find" This book reaches a whole new level for a compelling read.

Available at: wisdompresspublishing.com
and www.truelife-solutions.com

.

$14.95 plus $4 shipping within the United States.

Also available at Amazon.com and Barns and Noble.com

For more information call 866-612-7051

## Sounds of the Soul CD

The Angelic Tones that Balance
Brain Waves

Sounds of the Soul were channeled
from the celestial realm. Cutting edge
scientific studies are now being done
with neuro-feedback EEGs and the initial
findings are astounding. This CD when listened to through headphones
seems to balance Alpha, Beta, Theta, and Delta brain waves. The
implications of this are bound- less and, as we know, meditation has
the ability to decrease blood pressure and stress levels. We also know
that Sounds of the Soul may potentially normalize brain function and,
in doing so, heal the body on a cellular and soul level. Open your heart
and breathe in the music.

The sounds and tones are very relaxing and channel directly to the
soul. Many have experienced a reconnection with spirit and accelerated
. healing. There are 2 tracks on this CD. One is 18:50 min and the other
is

27:24 minutes.

Available at: wisdompresspublishing.com
and www.truelife-solutions.com
listen to a free clip of the CD on line.
$15 plus $4 shipping within the United States.

Also available at Amazon.com and Barns and Noble.com

For more information call 866-612-7051

## Also by Sheila Z. Stirling:

### Journey Meditation CD

This CD has two meditations on it. The first is a grounding and centering meditation and followed by a healing journey meditation.

The total time of this CD is about 25 minutes.

Available at: wisdompresspublishing.com
and www.truelife-solutions.com

.

$15 plus $4 shipping within the United States.

For more information call 866-612-7051

## Also by Sheila Z. Stirling:

### Deep Healing Meditation with Sounds of the Soul CD

This is a journey meditation that encourages your connection to the healer within. Building the healing energy of the cosmos and being in the heightened vibrations of the angelic realms from Sounds of the Soul.

This meditation is about 27 minutes.

Available at: wisdompresspublishing.com and www.truelife-solutions.com

Deep healing meditation guided by
Sheila Z. Stirling

$19.95 plus $4 shipping within the United States.

Also available at Amazon.com and Barns and Noble.com

For more information call 866-612-7051

Breinigsville, PA USA
12 July 2010
241630BV00005B/1/P